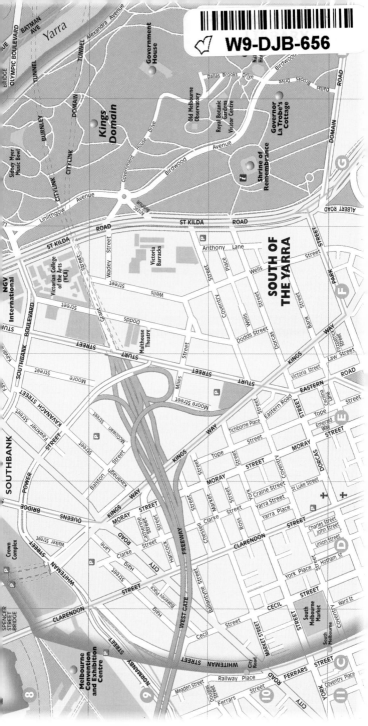

Fodor's
25 Best

MELBOURNE

How to Use
This Book

KEY TO SYMBOLS	
✚ Map reference to the accompanying fold-out map	🛳 Nearest riverboat or ferry stop
✉ Address	♿ Facilities for visitors with disabilities
☎ Telephone number	❓ Other practical information
🕒 Opening/closing times	▷ Further information
🍴 Restaurant or café	ℹ Tourist information
🚆 Nearest rail station	✋ Admission charges: Expensive (over A$25), Moderate (A$15–A$25) and Inexpensive (under A$15)
Ⓜ Nearest Metro (subway) station	
🚌 Nearest bus or tram route	

This guide is divided into four sections

● Essential Melbourne: An introduction to the city and tips on making the most of your stay.

● Melbourne by Area: We've broken the city into five areas, and recommended the best sights, shops, entertainment venues, nightlife and restaurants in each one. Suggested walks help you to explore on foot. Farther Afield takes you out of the city.

● Where to Stay: The best hotels, whether you're looking for luxury, budget or something in between.

● Need to Know: The info you need to make your trip run smoothly, including getting about by public transportation, weather tips, emergency phone numbers and useful websites.

Navigation In the Melbourne by Area chapter, we've given each area its own color, which is also used on the locator maps throughout the book and the map on the inside front cover.

Maps The fold-out map with this book is a comprehensive street plan of Melbourne. The grid on this fold-out map is the same as the grid on the locator maps within the book. We've given grid references within the book for each sight and listing.

Contents

Introducing Melbourne

Melbourne's obsession with music, art, food and sport make it pulse for locals and visitors alike. It's a forward-looking city that has a strong mixed cultural heritage. Welcome to the state capital of Victoria—one of the world's most vibrant cities.

Divided by the quiet waters of the Yarra River, Melbourne is the country's second-largest city after Sydney, with 4.9 million people, bringing together more than 200 nationalities. Its rich Indigenous history, mid-19th-century turn as goldfields gateway, and waves of post-World War II European migrants have ensured that the Melbourne of today exudes a fabulous multicultural air. The city also celebrates a long Chinese heritage combined with arrivals from Vietnam, India and Sri Lanka, and many African countries.

Thousands of cafés and restaurants serve cuisines from far and wide, complemented by the nation's best wines, many of which are produced in Victoria. Great shopping can be found in the city laneways and inner suburbs of Carlton, Fitzroy, South Yarra and Richmond. And only an hour or two's drive from the city you can see Australia's unique wildlife in the picturesque Dandenong Ranges or on the sandy beaches of Phillip Island.

Living in the sporting and cultural capital of Australia, Melburnians are as passionate about sport as they are about the arts. The unique Australian Rules Football (AFL) code had its origins here and the city is conversely home to Australia's finest art collection— the National Gallery of Victoria.

Melbourne has always been an important meeting place for the Indigenous Australian Kulin Nation and this book acknowledges the traditional custodians of Melbourne, the Wurundjeri of the Kulin Nation. *Wominjeka yearmann koondee biik Wurundjeri balluk*—welcome to the land of the Wurundjeri people.

FACTS AND FIGURES

- The most common language spoken after English is Mandarin (4 percent)
- Residents born overseas: 40 percent
- All city center trams in Melbourne are free
- First city outside of Europe and the US to host the Olympic Games, in 1956
- Maximum temperature recorded was 46.4 degrees Celsius (116°F) in 2009

MELBOURNE CUP

On the first Tuesday of November, Australia comes to a standstill, as people are glued to television sets to watch the nation's richest and most prestigious horse race, the Melbourne Cup. Run over 3,200m (2 miles), this handicap race carries prize money in excess of A$7 million. The day is a public holiday in Melbourne and most of Victoria.

FAMOUS MELBURNIANS

Melbourne is most famous for comedian Barry Humphries, feminist writer Germaine Greer, wildlife expert Steve Irwin, actors Cate Blanchett and Chris Hemsworth, and singers Kylie Minogue, Missy Higgins and Tina Arena. The city has produced some of Australia's top sportspeople, too, including aerial skier Alisa Camplin, tennis player Pat Cash and spin bowler Shane Warne.

GETTING AROUND

The metropolitan region of Melbourne is vast, around 80km (50 miles) north–south and 50km (31 miles) east–west. Since there is often some distance between the important sights, acquaint yourself with the city's trams, which provide a first-rate service. Melbourne's bike-share system is also great for short trips. See Getting Around (▷ 119) for more.

A Short Stay in Melbourne

DAY 1

Morning Have an early breakfast and walk to the **Royal Botanic Gardens** (▷ 60–61) for a quiet stroll around the grounds or perhaps punting on the lake. You might detour to the nearby **Shrine of Remembrance** (▷ 64), from where you have a fine vista back toward the city.

Mid-morning Hop on the St. Kilda Road tram that runs to the city and alight just over the Yarra River at Federation Square. Here you'll find the **Ian Potter Centre: NGV Australia** (▷ 46), the **Australian Centre for the Moving Image** (▷ 49) and the nearby park, Birrarung Marr.

Lunch Head along Russell Street to **Chinatown** (▷ 24) for dumplings at one of the many dining options and take a look at the **Chinese Museum** (▷ 24).

Afternoon Continue to Spring Street and check out the old **Princess Theatre** (▷ 31) and **Parliament House** (▷ 74–75), the grandiose home to Australia's first government, before arriving at the classic old **Windsor Hotel** (▷ 31), where you can enjoy a sumptuous afternoon tea.

Dinner Hop on the City Circle Tram and alight at Flinders Street station. Walk over Princes Bridge to **Southbank** (▷ 62), where you'll find an array of dining options from a range of multicultural cuisines; most restaurants have river and city views.

Evening Just nearby, on St. Kilda Road, is **The Arts Centre** (▷ 56), where you can choose a cultural night out from a range of opera, musical and drama performances.

DAY 2

Morning Walk around the CBD and head for **Hosier Lane** (▷ 44–45). Take a coffee break at **Higher Ground** (▷ 37–38) and have an inventive breakfast.

Mid-morning Walk to the vibrant **Queen Victoria Market** (▷ 28), where you can look for bargain clothing and souvenirs. One section of the market is devoted to food, so you can buy some tasty treats for a picnic lunch.

Lunch Take the tram to **St. Kilda** (▷ 97) for a picnic lunch on the seashore. Walk along The Esplanade—there's an arts and crafts market here on Sundays (10am–4pm)—then head to nearby Acland Street's array of tempting pastry shops for a coffee break.

Afternoon Return via tram to the city and visit the **SEA LIFE Melbourne Aquarium** (▷ 48), one of the city's most popular attractions, where you can see and touch a variety of marine creatures and dive with sharks. Take a tea break at the aquarium's Adventurer's Café, then walk back to **Federation Square** (▷ 42–43) to people-watch.

Dinner The free City Circle Tram will take you to **NewQuay** (▷ 25) in the Docklands precinct, where you can choose from a wide range of waterside restaurants on NewQuay Promenade. Get on board the **Melbourne Star** (▷ 25) observation wheel for some outstanding views of the city and bay.

Evening Walk back into the city for some great nightspots, including **Bird's Basement** (▷ 36) for jazz, funk and R&B acts. Head across to the **Gin Palace** (▷ 36) to finish up in style with a classic martini.

Top 25

ESSENTIAL MELBOURNE. TOP 25

8

These pages are a quick guide to the Top 25, which are described in more detail later. Here they are listed alphabetically, and the tinted background shows which area they are in.

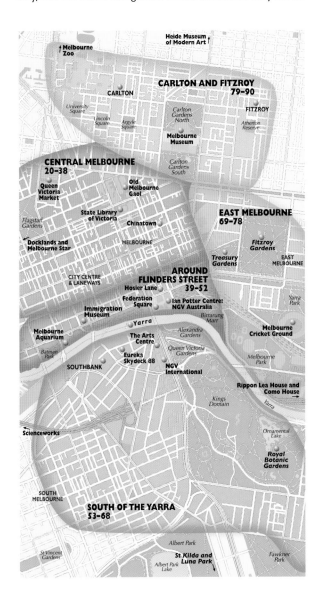

Heide Museum of Modern Art

Melbourne Zoo

CARLTON AND FITZROY
79–90

CARLTON

University Square

Carlton Gardens North

FITZROY

Lincoln Square

Argyle Square

Atherton Reserve

Melbourne Museum

CENTRAL MELBOURNE
20–38

Queen Victoria Market

Old Melbourne Gaol

Carlton Gardens South

State Library of Victoria

Chinatown

Flagstaff Gardens

EAST MELBOURNE
69–78

Fitzroy Gardens

Docklands and Melbourne Star

MELBOURNE

CITY CENTRE & LANEWAYS

Treasury Gardens

EAST MELBOURNE

AROUND FLINDERS STREET
39–52

Hosier Lane

Yarra Park

Federation Square

Ian Potter Centre: NGV Australia

Immigration Museum

Birrarung Marr

Melbourne Cricket Ground

Yarra

Melbourne Aquarium

The Arts Centre

Alexandra Gardens

Batman Park

Eureka Skydeck 88

Queen Victoria Gardens

Melbourne Park

SOUTHBANK

NGV International

Rippon Lea House and Como House

Kings Domain

Yarra

Scienceworks

Ornamental Lake

Royal Botanic Gardens

SOUTH MELBOURNE

SOUTH OF THE YARRA
53–68

St Vincent Gardens

Albert Park

St Kilda and Luna Park

Fawkner Park

Albert Park Lake

Shopping

Melburnians love to shop and the great array of retail outlets, from budget to upper end, attests to this. In fact, this city really is the shopping capital of Australia.

Australiana
Original Australian design tends to be influenced by nature. Natural materials such as indigenous timbers are used to produce utilitarian bowls and decorative sculptures, regional clays are used in pottery, and wool is often crafted into what could best be described as "wearable art." When it comes to jewelry, Australian opals are much admired and reputable dealers seek to educate potential buyers by displaying rough stones and exhibits explaining how opals are mined. Lustrous South Sea pearls, in all sizes, are great buys, as are gemstones set in Australian gold, and the distinctive pink Argyle diamonds. Check out several shops before settling on a purchase.

Out and About
Melbourne's retail heart may be the streets and laneways of the CBD, but in a variety of nearby suburbs you'll find interesting specialty shops selling clothing, giftware, souvenirs, books, music and jewelry, plus any number of art galleries. Interesting retail arcades around the city include The Block Arcade, Australia on Collins, Collins Place, Melbourne Central, Melbourne's GPO and the Royal Arcade. Seek out the quirky little stores in the laneways specializing in handmade jewelry, one-off chic designs, chocolates and unusual gifts. International brand names

BARGAIN SHOPPING

The post-Christmas season, from late December into January, is bargain shopping time. So is midwinter, in June and July. You can shop for clothing on a budget at any time in department and chain stores. Head to Richmond, where shops selling designer seconds and other well-priced clothes are plentiful. Inner-city suburbs offer bargains in secondhand clothing and many other items.

From cuddly toys to quirky clothes, Aboriginal objects to handmade hats—shopping Melbourne style

are available from the big retail stores Myer and David Jones, as well as from shops at the upper end of Collins Street and in South Yarra and Toorak. Be sure to trawl colorful Brunswick Street in Fitzroy and adjacent Smith Street for edgy fashions and homeware, secondhand goods, books and alternative art.

Head for a Bargain
For discount retailing, start at the Queen Victoria Market (▷ 28) on Queen Street. Bridge Road and Swan Street in Richmond offer designer seconds and well-priced clothes are plentiful. Be sure to check out the Sunday arts and crafts markets at the Arts Centre and St. Kilda Esplanade. The Prahran Market (▷ 66) also has fresh fruit and vegetables, and deli goods including organic produce—great for a picnic. High Street in Armadale has many antique dealers and art galleries.

If you have some extra time, make the trip to the nearby attractive town of Daylesford, where one of Victoria's largest outdoor markets is held at the old railway station.

Shopping Hours
Shops in the city and in designated shopping areas are generally open 10–6 on Monday to Thursday and Saturday to Sunday, and 10–9 on Friday. Individual hours do vary, so call ahead or check their website, especially on weekends.

BOOKS ON AUSTRALIA

To find out what the city was like in the 19th century, read *The Rise and Fall of Marvellous Melbourne* by Graeme Davidson. A powerful history of race relations since colonization is *Aboriginal Australians* by Richard Broome. For a brilliant travel guide to Indigenous Australia, pick up *Welcome to Country* by Marcia Langton. Tim Flannery's *The Future Eaters* is a fascinating ecological history of Australia. For first settlement encounters between Europeans and Indigenous Australians, read Inga Clendinnen's *Dancing With Strangers*. Read a collection of short memoirs in *Growing Up Aboriginal in Australia*, edited by Anita Heiss.

Shopping by Theme

Whether you're looking for a department store, a designer boutique, or something in between, you'll find it all in Melbourne. On this page shops are listed by theme. For a more detailed write-up, see the individual listings in Melbourne by Area.

Australiana
Craft Victoria (▷ 50)
MCG Shop (▷ 77)
Original & Authentic Aboriginal Art (▷ 35)
Queen Victoria Market (▷ 28)
R. M. Williams (▷ 35)

Books and Music
Chapel Street Bazaar (▷ 65)
City Basement Books (▷ 50)
Greville Records (▷ 65)
Hill of Content (▷ 34)
Kay Craddock (▷ 34)
Music Swop Shop (▷ 88)
Polyester (▷ 88)
Readings (▷ 88)
Syber's Books (▷ 66)

Fashion
Bonds Outlet (▷ 77)
The Cats Meow (▷ 50)
City Hatters (▷ 50)
Dakota 501 (▷ 65)
Le Louvre (▷ 65)
Retrostar Vintage Clothing (▷ 50)

Food and Drink
A1 Lebanese Bakery (▷ 104)
De Bortoli Winery (▷ 104)
Haigh's Chocolates (▷ 65)
Koko Black (▷ 88)
The Original Lolly Store (▷ 88)
Richmond Hill Café and Larder (▷ 77)
Simon Johnson: Toorak (▷ 65)
Sugar Station (▷ 50)
TarraWarra Winery (▷ 104)

Jewelry and Gems
Ashley Opals (▷ 34)
Keshett (▷ 34–35)

Markets
Camberwell Sunday Market (▷ 104)
Prahran Market (▷ 66)
Queen Victoria Market (▷ 28)
Rose Street Artists' Market (▷ 88)
St. Kilda Esplanade Market (▷ 104)
South Melbourne Market (▷ 66)
Sunday Art Market (▷ 66)

Shopping Centers
The Block Arcade (▷ 34)
Chadstone Shopping Centre (▷ 104)
Collins Street "Paris End" (▷ 34)
David Jones (▷ 34)
Jam Factory (▷ 65)
Melbourne Central (▷ 35)
Myer (▷ 35)
Royal Arcade (▷ 35)
Southgate (▷ 66)

Specialist Shops
Armadale Antique Centre (▷ 104)
Australian Geographic Shop (▷ 34)
Crumpler (▷ 50)
Dinosaur Designs (▷ 65)
Il Papiro (▷ 50)
Make Designed Objects (▷ 88)
National Wool Museum Shop (▷ 104)
NGV Design Store (▷ 65–66)
Post Industrial Design (▷ 104)
Wunderkammer (▷ 35)
Zetta Florence (▷ 88)

Tours
Go Get Around (▷ 35)
Outlet Shopping Tours (▷ 35)

Melbourne by Night

Melbourne's diverse nightlife has something for everyone—from the high arts of opera, classical music and cutting-edge theater to a night on the town at a club or pub.

Cultural Melbourne

The Arts Centre (▷ 56) presents excellent opera, ballet and classical music performances. The orchestra performs at Hamer Hall, the State Theatre hosts opera, and the center's Playhouse presents a variety of theatrical productions. Classical music concerts are also given at the Melbourne Town Hall, Melbourne University's Conservatorium of Music and the Sidney Myer Music Bowl. Lavish musicals can be enjoyed in Melbourne's fabulous old theaters, such as The Princess (▷ 31) and Her Majesty's, while the Athenaeum (▷ 30) hosts many comedy festival acts.

Out on the Town

For that special night out you'll find national and international stars performing at the Crown Entertainment Complex (▷ 62), Rod Laver Arena (▷ 75), The Forum (▷ 51) and the Melbourne Recital Centre (▷ 67).

LGBT Melbourne

Melbourne has a vibrant LGBT scene, especially in St. Kilda, South Yarra and Collingwood. An annual celebration of gay culture is held during January and February at Midsumma Festival (midsumma.org.au) and The Melbourne Queer Film Festival (mqff.com.au) is the oldest in the country, running for a couple of weeks in March. Check out timeout.com/melbourne/lgbt for events.

Dazzling scenes of Melbourne illuminated at night

GETTING HOME LATE AT NIGHT

While trams stop running at around midnight–1am from Sunday to Thursday, they continue all night on Friday and Saturday. The Nightrider bus service and suburban trains run all night too on weekends. Buy a myki card to use on all public transportation (▷ 118).

Where to Eat

People from more than 200 nations make Melbourne their home, so there may be some truth in the maxim that you can eat your way around the world here. The city has thousands of restaurants, most offering a range of Victoria's fine wines.

Home Talent
Australian chefs have made a name for themselves worldwide and Modern Australian, which fuses European and Asian food styles with local ingredients, is a big hit. Melbourne has also taken on Mexican and it's as authentic as it can get at the city's many cantinas. Dishes incorporating Aboriginal foods containing bush tucker ingredients have their own unique flavor. There are plenty of Greek and Italian restaurants, and, not surprisingly, seafood is popular in this bayside city. Local specialties include Melbourne rock oysters, kingfish, huge prawns, Tasmanian scallops and South Australian tuna. Appropriately, many seafood restaurants have waterfront locations, where you can buy excellent fish and chips to take away—St. Kilda, NewQuay and Williamstown are great spots for alfresco dining.

Melbourne's Asian Restaurants
The city's best Chinese cuisine is at the pinnacle of quality, along with refined cuisine from Japan, India, Indonesia, Burma, Korea, Laos and other Asian countries. The best Thai restaurants are equal to those found anywhere outside Thailand. Thai dishes are light and tasty—made with fresh produce and delicate spices and herbs. Vietnamese cuisine rivals Thai cuisine in popularity.

HOME GROWN
Victoria has a strong rural industry supplying prime beef and lamb, all types of seafood, and fresh fruit and vegetables. Dairy produce, in the form of specialty cheeses and yoghurts, is particularly worth seeking out. Restaurants draw on this produce for their ingredients.

Dining alfresco is a popular pastime for Melburnians and visitors alike

Where to Eat by Cuisine

There are places to eat to suit all tastes and budgets in Melbourne. On this page they are listed by cuisine. For a more detailed description of each venue, see Melbourne by Area.

Asia & the Middle East:
Chinese
Flower Drum (▷ 37)
Indian
Horn Please (▷ 106)
Israeli
Miznon (▷ 38)
Japanese
Izakaya Den (▷ 38)
Kenzan (▷ 52)
Kisumé Japanese (▷ 52)
Saké Restaurant Hamer Hall (▷ 68)
Korean
Hwaro Korean BBQ (▷ 38)
Malaysian
Blue Chillies (▷ 90)
Laksa King (▷ 106)
Thai
Cookie (▷ 36)
Long Chim (▷ 68)
Vietnamese
Coda Bar & Restaurant (▷ 52)
Tran Tran (▷ 78)

Cafés
Brunetti (▷ 52)
City Wine Shop (▷ 37)
Good Egg (▷ 68)

Hard Pressed Coffee (▷ 78)
Heart Attack and Vine (▷ 90)
Higher Ground (▷ 37–38)
Pellegrini's Espresso Bar (▷ 38)

Contemporary
Atlas Dining (▷ 68)
Attica (▷ 106)
Cumulus Inc (▷ 52)
The Deck (▷ 68)
Donovans (▷ 106)
Epocha (▷ 90)
Meatball & Wine Bar (▷ 78)
Spirit of Melbourne Dinner Cruise (▷ 68)
Tramcar Restaurant (▷ 52)

European:
Fish and chips
Hooked Fitzroy (▷ 90)
French
France Soir (▷ 68)
Noir (▷ 78)
Greek
Bahari (▷ 78)
Hella Good (▷ 52)

Italian
D.O.C. Espresso (▷ 90)
Tiamo (▷ 90)
Pizza
Baby Pizza (▷ 78)
Harley & Rose (▷ 106)
Sicilian
Rosa's Canteen (▷ 38)
Spanish/Portugese
Bar Lourinha (▷ 37)
MoVida Aqui (▷ 38)

Out of Town
The Healesville Hotel (▷ 106)
Sky High Restaurant (▷ 106)
Vue Grand Hotel (▷ 106)

South American & Mexican
Mamasita (▷ 38)
Mesa Verde (▷ 36)
Onda (▷ 78)

Vegetarian
Smith & Daughters (▷ 90)
Vegie Bar (▷ 90)

Top Tips For...

These great suggestions will help you tailor your ideal visit to Melbourne, no matter how you choose to spend your time. Each sight or listing has a fuller write-up elsewhere in the book.

EATING OUT

Classic Italian dishes are prepared at **D.O.C.** (▷ 90) in Little Italy.
Cantonese cuisine can be sampled at the elegant **Flower Drum** (▷ 38) in Chinatown.
The free City Circle Tram will take you to **NewQuay** (▷ 26), where you can choose from a range of waterside restaurants.
Explore the laneways and stop in for tapas at **Bar Tini** (▷ 51) on **Hosier Lane** (▷ 44–45).

SPECTATOR SPORTS

Catch an Aussie Rules football game at the **Melbourne Cricket Ground** (▷ 73).
Rod Laver Arena (▷ 75) is the home of tennis—if you are in the city while it's taking place in January, get tickets to the Australian Open.
Head to the bubbled dome of **AAMI Stadium** (▷ 75) to see soccer and rugby.

FREE THINGS

At the Royal Botanic Gardens (▷ 60–61) you can stroll among the plant collections or take in an open-air performance.
See paintings, sculptures and decorative arts at the **NGV International** (▷ 58–59).
Go to the **Abbotsford Convent** (▷ 98) arts precinct for galleries, exhibitions and weekend markets.

STAYING AT BUDGET HOTELS

At the **Space Hotel** (▷ 109) rooms cost around A$100 per night. There's a sundeck with a spa.
Near the Princess Theatre is **City Limits** (▷ 109), in the heart of the Melbourne CBD.
Stay at the **Tolarno hotel** (▷ 109) in St. Kilda, once the private residence of Melbourne artist Mirka Mora.

Clockwise from top left: Hosier Lane; Ian Potter Centre; Transport Hotel, Federation Square; Scienceworks

LOCAL CULTURE

The nation's best collection of Australian art can be found in the **Ian Potter Centre** (▷ 46) at Federation Square.

Koorie Heritage Trust (▷ 49) features works by contemporary Aboriginal artists.

The **Immigration Museum** (▷ 47) hosts community festivals showcasing the music and culture of people from around the world.

Learn about Aboriginal law and knowledge at the **Bunjilaka Aboriginal Cultural Centre** (▷ 84).

GOING OUT ON THE TOWN

Head to Chloe's Bar at **Young and Jacksons** (▷ 51) to admire the famous nude portrait, and to enjoy a craft beer or cider.

The **Transport Hotel** (▷ 51) has live music and DJs every night of the week.

Taste a rare single malt at **Whisky & Alement** (▷ 37) or a Bartender's Choice cocktail at **The Everleigh** (▷ 89).

ENTERTAINING THE KIDS

Scienceworks (▷ 98) has lots of hands-on exhibits—don't miss the Lightning Room.

The Fire Services Museum (▷ 74) has a collection of restored fire trucks.

Take the kids to the interactive and forest displays in the **Melbourne Museum** (▷ 84–85).

Let them be a pirate for the morning at the tall-ship **Polly Woodside** (▷ 64).

Go cuddle guinea pigs at the **Collingwood Children's Farm** (▷ 99).

BEER & ROOFTOP GARDENS

The **Mitre Tavern** (▷ 37) holds records as the oldest pub with the biggest city beer garden.

Arbory Bar & Eatery (▷ 51) wins the longest beer garden, running alongside Flinders Street Station and the Yarra for 100 meters!

Madame Brussels (▷ 36) takes rooftop to another level with its kitchy terraced cocktail bar.

Naked for Satan (▷ 89) has killer views of Fitzroy and the city.

Museum; Space Hotel; AAMI; Rod Laver Arena

A NIGHT OUT AT THE THEATER

See a show at **La Mama Theatre** (▷ 89), then head to Lygon Street for an after-theater drink. See opera and ballet at the **State Theatre** (▷ 67) in the Arts Centre or comedy and book launches at the **Athenaeum** (▷ 30).
For something a bit different, the innovative **Malthouse Theatre** (▷ 67) is the place to go.

A WALK ON THE WILD SIDE

Phillip Island (▷ 102) has a substantial water-bird population and there are elevated boardwalks through bushland for easy viewing. The **Dandenong Ranges** (▷ 101) are less than an hour's drive from the CBD, and have lots of walking trails and great birdlife.
Wildlife park **Healesville Sanctuary** (▷ 101) is set in the foothills of the scenic Yarra Valley. Home to plenty of Australian wildlife, **Melbourne Zoo** (▷ 95) has a world-class gorilla enclosure.

CUTTING-EDGE ARCHITECTURE

The 10-story university building, **RMIT Design Hub** (▷ 31), incorporates all aspects of sustainability in its all-embracing eco design.
Eureka Skydeck 88 (▷ 57) is the observation deck at the top of the Eureka Tower and offers panoramic views of Melbourne and surrounds.

SEEING LIVE MUSIC

Check out one of the city's live music institutions: the rock 'n' roll **Corner Hotel** (▷ 77), **Cherry Bar** (▷ 51) or **Prince Bandroom** (▷ 105).
The Forum (▷ 51) is a bigger venue but with no less personality.

A CITY OF LITERATURE

In 2008 Melbourne became a City of Literature and the **Wheeler Centre** (▷ 31) was founded, a hub for writing and ideas.
Next door, the **State Library of Victoria** (▷ 29) has over 2 million books.
Indie bookstore **Readings** (▷ 88) is a book-lover's haven and meeting place.

Melbourne leisure—Melbourne Arts Centre; a lowland gorilla at Melbourne Zoo; the striking Eureka Tower; The Forum

Melbourne by Area

Central Melbourne

Jump on the City Circle Tram and explore Central Melbourne's grid-planned laneways and waterfront, chock-full of restaurants, cafés, bars and malls, and the high-rises that play host to a central business district.

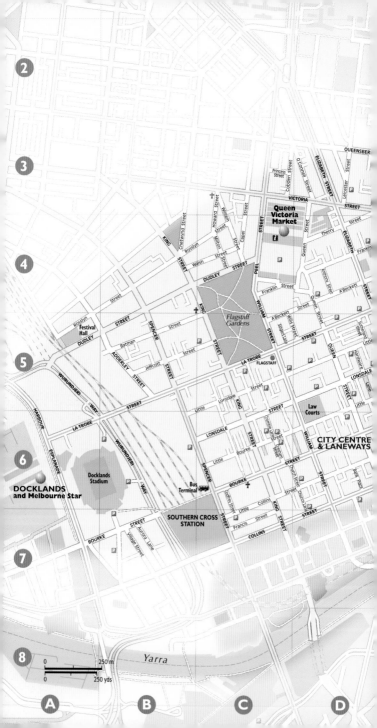

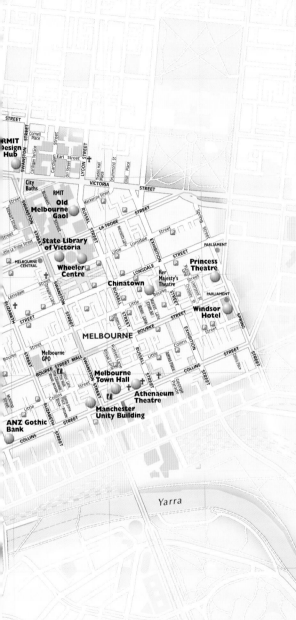

STREET

RMIT Design Hub

Cornell Place

Cardigan Terrace

Cardigan Earl Street

SWANSTON STREET

LYGON STREET

Trades Hall Place

Drummond St

VICTORIA

City Baths

RMIT

Mackenzie Street

VICTORIA STREET

Bowen Crescent

Old Melbourne Gaol

SWANSTON STREET

RUSSELL STREET

LA TROBE

LA TROBE STREET

Little La Trobe Street

Kenneth Lane

Lonsdale

street

Spring Street

State Library of Victoria

MELBOURNE CENTRAL

Wheeler Centre

Little

Lonsdale

LONSDALE

Exhibition

PARLIAMENT

Princess Theatre

Chinatown

SWANSTON STREET

ELIZABETH STREET

Lonsdale

RUSSELL

STREET

Her Majesty's Theatre

Waratah Lane

Liverpool St

Crossley St

bourne

STREET

PARLIAMENT

Windsor Hotel

Bourke

MELBOURNE

Crossley St

BOURKE STREET

Bourke STREET

RUSSELL

Little

EXHIBITION

SPRING STREET

Melbourne GPO

BOURKE STREET MALL

Royal Lane

SWANSTON STREET

Collins

COLLINS STREET

Melbourne Town Hall

STREET

Little Collins

George Parade

Collins

Athenaeum Theatre

ELIZABETH STREET

ANZ Gothic Bank

Little

Manchester Unity Building

COLLINS

Yarra

E   F   G

Chinatown

The streets behind the stone lions, where the city's Chinatown comes alive on carnival day

THE BASICS

chinatownmelbourne.com.au

➕ F5

✉ Little Bourke Street (east)

🍴 Many restaurants

🚉 Parliament

🚋 City Circle Tram

Chinese Museum

chinesemuseum.com.au

➕ F5

✉ 22 Cohen Place

☎ 9662 2888

🕐 Daily 10–4

🚉 Parliament

🚋 City Circle Tram

♿ Moderate

💲 Inexpensive

❓ Guided/audiovisual tours

HIGHLIGHTS

● Chinese Museum
● Dumpling houses
● Flower Drum restaurant (▷ 37)
● Archway

TIP

● Explore the laneways to find hidden restaurants.

You can't miss the majestic gold, red and neon archways that invite you into the heritage laneways of Melbourne's Chinatown. Yum cha and dumplings await, hidden above a colorful medley of bars, herbalists and duty-free shops.

The laneways Two stone lions mark this part of Little Bourke Street, between Exhibition and Swanston streets, although it spills over into the adjoining streets and lanes. After the 1850s gold rush, many Chinese immigrants opened shops, furniture factories and other businesses here, and some of the 19th-century Victorian buildings still stand.

Chinese New Year The laneways go off like firecrackers as dancing Chinese lions scare away evil spirits, while musical and cultural performances fill the big stage. Celebrations hit a high when over 200 people carry the enormous Dai Loong Dragon through the streets to the beat of drums.

Chinese Museum Go back in time and follow the journey of Chinese immigrants on a walk-through goldfields re-creation and have your fortune told in the temple of Guan Gong. The Millennium Dragon lives here too—it's reputedly the world's largest processional dragon and is paraded each year at the Moomba Festival in March, a weekend community carnival with parades, fireworks and the hilarious Birdman Rally on the Yarra.

Docklands and Melbourne Star

Docklands is the city's waterfront area, with restaurants, galleries and shops set alongside the Yarra River and Victoria Harbour. Over the stunning pedestrian Webb Bridge, art, ice skating and an observation wheel await.

Art trail Featuring local and international artists, the Harbourside art trail has more than 30 works and takes you through Dockland's promenades and parklands, over scenic walkways and on to marinas. On NewQuay Promenade, Melbourne artist Adrian Mauriks' *Silence* sets the scene, the huge, smooth, white sculptures arousing imaginations. In contrast, tucked away near La Trobe Street, the geometric wooden blocks of Antony Gormley's *Cast IV* leave you feeling exposed. And then there's John Kelly's surreal *Cow Up A Tree*.

NewQuay At the northwestern edge of the harbor, NewQuay Promenade has many restaurants offering a wide range of cuisines, as well as plenty of cafés and bars—all with stunning harbor and city views. Many seasonal events take place in the public Piazza, and the huge District shopping center sits just behind.

Melbourne Star The 120m (394-foot) observation wheel has 360-degree views as far as the Dandenong Ranges and Port Phillip Bay, and is wheelchair friendly. Double the fun and sign up for the Skate & Fly package at the O'Brien Group Arena ice rink next door.

THE BASICS

whatson.melbourne.vic.gov.au
+ A6
⊠ Harbour Esplanade
🕑 Daily until late
🍽 Many fine restaurants
🚆 Southern Cross
🚋 City Circle Tram; tram 11, 30, 48, 70, 86
♿ Good
💲 Free

Melbourne Star
melbournestar.com
+ A6
⊠ 101 Waterfront Way
☎ 9658 9658
🕑 May–Aug daily 11–7; Sep–Apr daily 11–10
🍽 Star Departure Lounge
🚆 Southern Cross
🚋 City Circle Tram; tram 11, 30, 48, 70, 86
♿ Very good
💲 Moderate
❓ In-cabin audio tour

HIGHLIGHTS

● NewQuay
● Ice skating
● Melbourne Star
● Public art

Old Melbourne Gaol

TOP 25

Ned Kelly's death mask (middle) on display at the notorious Old Melbourne Gaol

THE BASICS

oldmelbournegaol.com.au

✚ E4

✉ 377 Russell Street

☎ 9663 7228

🕐 Daily 9.30–5

🍴 Restaurants nearby

Ⓜ Melbourne Central

♿ Limited

💲 Expensive

❓ Hangman's Night Tours 8.30–9.30pm; Ghosts? What Ghosts! Night Tour 8.30–9.30pm; A Night in the Watch House Tour 9–10pm. All run on various nights.

HIGHLIGHTS

- Bluestone building
- Death masks
- Ned Kelly memorabilia
- Candlelight night tours
- Prisoners' Stories
- Being arrested

TIP

- Not recommended if you have very young children.

Prepare to be scared out of your wits by death masks and appalled at inmate stories. This historic bluestone prison is fixed in national folklore as the place where Australia's most famous bushranger, Ned Kelly, was hanged.

A gruesome past This grim, gloomy place, with thick walls, small cells and heavy iron doors, is Victoria's oldest surviving penal establishment. Begun in 1842 and completed in 1864, it consists of three levels of claustrophobic cells. The gallows, where 133 men and women were hanged, is the centerpiece of the complex. The death masks of some of those executed are on display, along with their stories. The most famous hanging was that of bushranger Ned Kelly, one of the nation's folk heroes, an outlaw executed in 1880, whose famous last words were, "Such is life." The present cell block was in use until 1929, when the last prisoners were transferred to other prisons.

In the cells The penal museum presents displays and provides information on many infamous inmates, displays the Hangman's Box with its original contents and chronicles incarcerations. The flogging frame is on view along with the punishment instruments.

Night terrors Nightly tours recreate the prison's gruesome past, some led by hangmen telling horrendous stories and frightening you with loud noises. Not for the faint hearted.

Queue Victoria Market

The array of mouth-watering produce on sale at the bustling Queen Victoria Market

THE BASICS

qvm.com.au

✚ C4

✉ Corner of Elizabeth and Victoria streets

☎ 9320 5822

🕐 Tue, Thu 6–2, Fri 6–5, Sat 6–3, Sun 9–4

🍴 Many cafés and restaurants nearby and plenty of stalls selling snack food and coffee

🚇 Melbourne Central

🚋 City trams 19, 57, 58 and 59

♿ Moderate

HIGHLIGHTS

● The stallholders
● Exotic tropical fruits
● Australian cheeses
● Historic buildings
● Market tours
● Night Market

DID YOU KNOW?

Queen Victoria Market was formerly a cemetery. There's a memorial passage on the corner of Queen and Therry streets.

A Melbourne institution and the city's most popular market, Vic Market is where food and culture collide in a chaotic collection of delicatessen and grocery stalls, florists, souvenirs, clothing, art and music.

History Just a few minutes' walk from the city center, this bustling, chaotic market, over 1,000 stalls on 7ha (17 acres), is Australia's largest. Established in 1878, many of the buildings date back to the 19th century, including the Meat Hall (1869), Sheds A to F (1878) and the two-story shops on Victoria Street (1887).

Markets The colorful traders are an attraction in their own right, promoting their wares and bantering with passersby. In the Lower Market are the Meat Hall, with meat, fish and game; the Dairy Hall, with delicatessens and bakeries; and a section with fresh fruit and vegetables, as well as a huge range of ready-to-eat foods. On a nearby rise, a stretch of open-sided sheds, known as the Upper Market, houses a wide variety of fresh produce, clothing and souvenirs. A seasonal Night Market runs on Wednesday nights from 5–10pm during summer (Nov–Mar) and winter (Jun–Aug).

Guided tours The Ultimate Foodie Tour provides a chance to taste Australian cheeses, nuts, preserves, meats and exotic tropical fruits, while learning about the market's original buildings and its fascinating past.

State Library of Victoria

Victoria's State Library is majestic inside and out. Besides more than 2 million books, maps and newspapers, the architecture is an attraction in its own right with an impressive domed reading room, spiral staircases and ornate galleries.

Magnificent reading rooms Six stories high, the La Trobe Reading Room is an octagonal domed space that dates back to 1913. Climb all the way up to level 6 for an awe-inspiring view of the books, desks adorned with antique green reading lamps and avid readers below. Architecturally magnificent in its own way, the Redmond Barry Reading Room is the largest, bookended by the library's magazine and journal collections, and sweeping marble staircases.

Library collections The library houses its own extensive collections of artwork. Permanent (and free) exhibitions on levels 4 and 5 contain everything from Aussie classics and medieval manuscripts to Ned Kelly's armor. The north and south rotundas hold 19th- and 20th-century artworks that capture the history of Victoria. Oil paintings and portrait sculpture can be found in the Cowen Gallery, and the Keith Murdoch Gallery often has touring exhibitions.

White Night festival at the library Each year White Night lights up buildings across the city. The domed ceiling comes alive with projected light and sound, and the library facade is transformed into a dreamy wonderland.

THE BASICS

slv.vic.gov.au
+ E4
✉ 328 Swanston Street
☎ 8664 7000
🕐 Mon–Thu 10–9, Fri–Sun 10–6
🍴 Mr Tulk ($$)
🚇 Melbourne Central
🚋 City Circle Tram
♿ Very good
🎫 Free
❓ The Welcome to the Library Tour runs Tue at 11am. There are other free tours every day, ask at the Trescowthick Information Centre.

HIGHLIGHTS

● La Trobe Reading Room
● Ned Kelly's Armor
● Dome to Catacomb Tour
● The Courtyards
● Redmond Barry Reading Room

TIP

● The library is huge so pick up a handy map from the information center.

More to See

ANZ GOTHIC BANK
This highly decorated Gothic revival bank, completed in 1887, has been compared to the Doge's Palace in Venice. Its magnificent interior, with gold-leaf ornamentation amid graceful arches and pillars, features decorative shields from the countries and cities that the original bank, the England, Scottish and Australian Bank, traded with.

➕ D6 ✉ 386 Collins Street ☎ 8655 5152 🕐 Mon–Fri 10–3 🚋 City Circle Tram 💵 Free

ATHENAEUM THEATRE
athenaeumtheatre.com.au
A big comedy festival venue, the Athenaeum has hosted the likes of local comedy hero Sammy J and Monty Python legend Michael Palin. You'll also find opera on the menu, and many a book launch has taken place on its historic stage.

➕ F6 ✉ 188 Collins Street ☎ 9650 1500 🕐 Mon–Fri 11am–midnight, Sat 12–12, Sun noon–11pm 🚋 City Circle Tram

MANCHESTER UNITY BUILDING
manchesterunitybuilding.com.au
Step back into 1932 and wander through the marble-floored arcade and up Melbourne's oldest escalator. Take a breakfast, lunch or cheese-and-wine tour to visit the turreted five-story Gothic-style tower on top, with breathtaking views of the city.

➕ E6 ✉ 220 Collins Street ☎ 9663 5494 🕐 Mon–Fri 7am–3pm 🍴 1932 Cafe 🚋 City Circle Tram ♿ Few 💵 Free; tours expensive

MELBOURNE TOWN HALL
melbourne.vic.gov.au/townhalltours
Take a Town Hall tour and visit the Chambers, see the Grand Organ and stand on the balcony where the Beatles stood back in 1964. Festivals, exhibitions, orchestral performances, theater and even wedding receptions all take place in this 19th-century building.

➕ F6 ✉ 90–120 Swanston Street ☎ 9658 9658 🕐 Tour only, Mon, Wed–Fri 11am and 1pm 🚋 City Circle Tram ♿ Few 💵 Free

Fusion architecture—the new towers over the old, ANZ Gothic Bank

The Princess Theatre

PRINCESS THEATRE

marrinergroup.com.au/venues/princess-theatre

One of the world's grand old theaters, The Princess was built in 1854. Today it mounts major musical productions. The Australian adaptation of *Harry Potter and the Cursed Child* is due to run here in 2019—the third opening of the play after London and New York.

E5 ✉ 163 Spring Street ☎ 9299 9800 ⊙ Daily 🍴 Bistro 🚋 City Circle Tram 💲 Free

RMIT DESIGN HUB

designhub.rmit.edu.au

This visionary design hub is a soaring 10-story building covered in circles of sandblasted glass that move with the sun and wind, helping to moderate the temperature of the building. The five-star energy building has a number of exhibition spaces that are open to the public.

E3 ✉ Corner of Victoria and Swanston streets ☎ 9925 2260 ⊙ Tue–Fri 10–5, Sat 12–5 🚋 City Circle Tram 💲 Free

WHEELER CENTRE

wheelercentre.com

A place for public conversation, you'll find that everything is discussed at this hub for writing and ideas. Talks at the Wheeler Centre are mostly free, plus there's book launches and readings, performances and major events.

E4 ✉ 176 Little Lonsdale Street ☎ 9094 7809 ⊙ Talk times vary 🚋 City Circle Tram ♿ Very good 💲 Free

WINDSOR HOTEL

thehotelwindsor.com.au

A Melbourne landmark listed by the National Trust and the grandest hotel in Australia, the meticulously restored Windsor has all the elegance of a luxury 19th-century hotel. Even if you don't stay here, pop in to admire the sweeping, wrought-iron staircase, the ornately detailed foyer and the rich detail of the Grand Ballroom.

G5 ✉ 111 Spring Street ☎ 9633 6000 ⊙ 24-hour reception 🚋 City Circle Tram 💲 Free for a look

Windsor Hotel

City Heritage Walk

Learn about Melbourne's fascinating past on this walk through the city's heritage precincts, streets, arcades and laneways.

DISTANCE: 4km (2.5 miles)   **ALLOW:** 3 hours

START

IMMIGRATION MUSEUM
(▷ 47)
🚉 D7 🚋 City Circle Tram

END

WINDSOR HOTEL (▷ 31)
🚉 G5 🚋 City Circle Tram

❶ Begin at the Immigration Museum and head for King Street, via William Street and Flinders Lane. Look for the bluestone buildings along the way, before turning into Collins Street.

❽ In Spring Street, visit the City Museum at Old Treasury (▷ 74), Parliament House (▷ 74 and pictured opposite) and the splendid Windsor Hotel (▷ 31).

❷ On Collins Street, right next to the Rialto Towers, check out the old Rialto Hotel and the nearby ornate 19th-century office buildings.

❼ Proceed down Collins Street toward Spring Street to see its three blocks of fine churches, theaters, stores and the exclusive Melbourne Club.

❸ Detour along William Street to Little Collins and back to Collins via Bank Place and pop into the Mitre Tavern (▷ 37).

❻ Head back to Swanston Street to admire the architecture of the Melbourne Town Hall (▷ 30) and the Manchester Unity Building (▷ 30) on the opposite corner of Collins Street.

❹ Back in Collins Street, view the ornate banking chamber of the ANZ Gothic Bank (▷ 30) and below it the Banking Museum.

❺ Just past Elizabeth Street, look for the entrance to The Block Arcade (▷ 34) and follow this covered shopping area through to the Royal Arcade (▷ 35) in Little Collins Street.

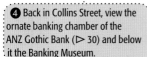

CENTRAL MELBOURNE WALK

Shopping

ASHLEY OPALS

ashleyopals.com.au

Jewelry made from an exclusive range of opal stones, Australian South Sea and Tahitian pearls, diamonds and precious gems. Staff can individually design pieces, or choose from an array of ready-made designs. ➕ F6 ✉ 85 Collins Street ☎ 9654 4866 🕐 Mon–Thu 10–6, Fri 10–7, Sat 10–5 🚋 City Circle Tram

AUSTRALIAN GEOGRAPHIC SHOP

shop.australiangeographic.com.au

Australia's best artists, writers, photographers, craftspeople and designers join forces to produce clothing, prints, stationery, birdhouses, telescopes and more for both kids and adults. ➕ E5 ✉ 287 Lonsdale Street ☎ 9639 5400 🕐 Sat–Wed 10–7, Thu & Fri 10–9 🚋 City Circle Tram

THE BLOCK ARCADE

theblock.com.au

Opened in 1892, this National Trust-classified arcade has an intricately tiled floor, decorative ironwork, stained-glass windows and 30 boutique shops and cafés. Find everything from antique jewelry to top-class chocolates and teas. ➕ E6 ✉ 282 Collins Street ☎ 9654 5244 🚋 City Circle Tram

COLLINS STREET ("PARIS END")

Many exclusive boutiques are along this elegant stretch of Collins Street, including the stylish and popular Collins Place center with its many specialist shops. ➕ G5 ✉ Collins Street 🚋 City Circle Tram

DAVID JONES

davidjones.com.au

Known as DJs, this department store sells quality goods. There is an excellent food hall in the Bourke Street shop—the lower level is one of the city's most exclusive. ➕ D6 ✉ Little Bourke, Bourke and Little Collins streets ☎ 9643 2222 🕐 Sun–Wed 9.30–7, Thu & Fri 9.30–9, Sat 9–7 🚋 City Circle Tram

HILL OF CONTENT

hillofcontentbookshop.com

Melbourne's oldest bookshop has a solid range of current titles and knowledgable staff can help you find the book you want. It's wall to wall books, both upstairs and downstairs. ➕ F5 ✉ 86 Bourke Street ☎ 9662 9472 🕐 Mon–Thu 9–6, Fri 9–8, Sat 10–6, Sun 11–5 🚋 Tram 86, 96

KAY CRADDOCK

kaycraddock.com

One of Melbourne's top secondhand and rare books dealers, with books dating from the 15th to the 21st century. Keep an eye out for the quirky collection of owl ornaments around the shop. ➕ E6 ✉ 156 Collins Street ☎ 9654 8506 🕐 Mon–Thu 10–6, Fri 10–7, Sat 10–4 🚋 City Circle Tram

KESHETT

keshett.com.au

This family-owned store sells both contemporary and antique jewelry

---

DELICACIES

Be sure to visit the Queen Victoria Market (▷ 28), where you can sample cheese from the Yarra Valley and Tasmania, and seafood from the cooler southern oceans—everything from scallops to Tasmanian smoked salmon. You'll also find the macadamia in plentiful supply, the only native nut to hit the world stage.

from the art deco, Edwardian, art nouveau and Victorian eras.

🔲 E6 ✉ 323 Collins Street ☎ 9654 1514 🚋 City Circle Tram

MELBOURNE CENTRAL

melbournecentral.com.au

Find over 300 specialist shops and eateries over five levels, housed around the 1889 Coops Shot Tower and topped by a glass cone designed by Japanese architect Kisho Kurokawa. The giant Marionette Watch in Shot Tower Square plays "Waltzing Matilda" on the hour.

🔲 E4 ✉ Corner of Swanston and La Trobe streets ☎ 9922 1122 🕐 Sat–Wed 10–7, Thu & Fri 10–9 🚇 Melbourne Central 🚋 City Circle Tram

MYER

myer.com.au

Starting out as the Myer Emporium in 1911, the biggest department store in the southern hemisphere sells a wide range of fashion, designer housewares, gifts and cosmetics.

🔲 D6 ✉ 314–336 Bourke Street ☎ 8609 7500 🕐 Sat–Wed 9.30–7, Thu & Fri 9.30–9 🚋 City Circle Tram

ORIGINAL & AUTHENTIC ABORIGINAL ART

originalandauthenticaboriginalart.com

Representing independent Aboriginal artists, this Aboriginal art gallery has traditional and contemporary works from the Kimberley and Arnhem Land.

🔲 F5 ✉ 90 Bourke Street ☎ 9663 5133 🕐 Mon–Sat 10–7, Sun 11–5 🚇 Parliament

R. M. WILLIAMS

rmwilliams.com.au

R.M. Williams made his first boot in 1932 and the legend of the "Craftsman" boot continues today. Find authentic Australian outback clothing, traditional Aussie footwear and a bespoke boot service, too.

🔲 E4 ✉ Melbourne Central, 300 Lonsdale Street ☎ 9663 7126 🕐 Sat–Wed 10–7, Thu & Fri 10–9 🚇 Melbourne Central 🚋 City Circle Tram

ROYAL ARCADE

royalarcade.com.au

Australia's oldest retail arcade still holds true to its Renaissance Revival style and giant statues Gog and Magog strike the hour as they did way back in 1892. The arcade has around 30 boutique shops that sell fashion and gifts.

🔲 E6 ✉ 335 Bourke Street Mall ☎ 0438 891 212 🕐 Mon–Thu 9–6, Fri 10–8, Sat 9–5, Sun 10–5 🚋 City Circle Tram

WUNDERKAMMER

wunderkammer.com.au

Curio shop Wunderkammer's glass cabinets display everything from insects and fossils to taxidermy and antique maps. The shop supports local artists and is a great place for a unique gift— just check you are able to take it home with you!

🔲 D5 ✉ 439 Lonsdale Street ☎ 9642 4694 🕐 Mon–Fri 10–6, Sat & Sun 10–4 🚋 City Circle Tram

SHOPPING TOURS

To explore out-of-the-way bargain shopping districts, you might want to call one of the following operators. Go Get Around (☎ 9579 5771, gogetaroundtours.com.au) specializes in warehouse shopping for clothing and other goods at wholesale prices. Outlet Shopping Tours (☎ 8822 4568, outletshoppingtours.com.au) offers smaller group tours to wholesalers.

Entertainment and Nightlife

BIRD'S BASEMENT

birdsbasement.com

Charlie Parker's New York Birdland hit Melbourne in the form of Bird's Basement. It gets packed Wednesday to Sunday with local and international jazz, funk and R&B acts so be sure to reserve ahead online. Head to Bird's Upstairs for dinner before a show.

 C5 ✉ 111 Singers Lane ☎ 1300 225 299 🕐 Wed–Sun from 7pm till late 🚉 Flagstaff

CITY BATHS

melbourne.vic.gov.au/melbournecitybaths

Open since 1860, this historic swimming complex is the place to get in a few laps or to just cool off on a hot day. Also has a gym, Jacuzzis, saunas and squash courts.

🔲 E4 ✉ 420 Swanston Street ☎ 9663 5888 🕐 Mon–Thu 6am–10pm, Fri 6am–8pm, Sat–Sun 8–6 🚋 Swanston Street Tram

COMEDY THEATRE

marrinergroup.com.au/venues/comedy-theatre

A delightful 1,000-seater theater modeled on a Florentine palace, hosting a variety of shows including *Waiting for Godot*, *The Rocky Horror Show* and *Avenue Q*. Enjoy a pre-show meal and cocktails with the show package.

🔲 F5 ✉ 240 Exhibition Street ☎ 9299 4950 🚋 City Circle Tram

CURTIN HOUSE

curtinhouse.com

"Vertical lane" Curtin House has six stories of entertainment. On the 1st and 2nd floors you'll find Thai bar/restaurant Cookie and live-music bar The Toff In Town. On the 6th floor is Mexican bar/restaurant Mesa Verde and up on the roof, you guessed it, Rooftop Bar.

🔲 E5 ✉ 252 Swanston Street 🕐 Daily noon–3am 🚋 Tram 1, 3, 5, 6, 16, 64, 67, 72

DOCKLANDS STADIUM

marvelstadium.com.au

Catch an AFL game at Docklands Stadium, home to AFL teams Essendon, Carlton, North Melbourne, St. Kilda and the mighty Western Bulldogs. Also hosts concerts and a variety of other sports.

🔲 A6 ✉ 740 Bourke Street ☎ 8625 7700 🕐 Call for details 🚋 City Circle Tram

GIN PALACE

ginpalace.com.au

Serious drinkers make their way to this basement bar for the classic martinis and the stylish ambience. There's a mind-boggling selection of gins on offer.

🔲 E6 ✉ 10 Russell Place ☎ 9654 0533 🕐 Daily 4pm–3am 🚋 City Circle Tram

HER MAJESTY'S THEATRE

hmt.com.au

Prepare for a night of indulgence. You'll be seated in lush velvet seats, while Her Majesty's lays on art deco luxury and the world's greatest musicals, ballet and opera. A romantic night out since 1866.

🔲 F5 ✉ 219 Exhibition Street ☎ 8643 3300 🚋 City Circle Tram

MADAME BRUSSELS

madamebrussels.com

A fun and kitschy terraced cocktail bar that overlooks the city, Madame Brussels offers a variety of punches served in jugs and delivered by staff dressed in tennis whites. Head back to The Parlour room to sample a rare rum.

BUYING A TICKET

At Half Tix, next door to the Melbourne Town Hall, you can get discounted tickets on the day of performance. Tickets must be bought in person and paid for in cash (Mon 10–2, Tue–Fri 11–6, Sat 10–4).

🚇 F5 ✉ 59 Bourke Street ☎ 9662 2775
🕐 Daily noon–1am 🚊 Tram 86, 96

MITRE TAVERN

mitretavern.com.au

Not only the oldest building in Melbourne, and a tavern for over 140 years, the Mitre breaks records with the biggest beer garden in the city too. Enjoy a beer with a steak at the Steakhouse restaurant.

🚇 D6 ✉ 5 Bank Place ☎ 9670 5644

🕐 Mon–Fri 11–midnight, Sat 12–12, Sun noon–11 🚊 City Circle Tram

WHISKY & ALEMENT

whiskyandale.com.au

Both novice and serious enthusiasts will enjoy the whiskey conversations here about the more than 1,000 types. If you're really serious, take a class.

🚇 F4 ✉ 270 Russell Street ☎ 9654 1284
🕐 Tue–Sat 4pm–1am, Sun & Mon 4–11pm
🚊 City Circle Tram

Where to Eat

enjoy wine and cheese—matured by the Spring Street Cheese Cellar next door.

🚇 G4 ✉ 159 Spring Street ☎ 9654 6657
🕐 Daily morning–midnight 🚊 City Circle Tram

FLOWER DRUM ($$$)

flower-drum.com

Flower Drum has been constantly creating and finessing Cantonese dishes since 1975. Led by head chef Anthony Lui, the menu is a seasonal delight of delicate flavors. Enjoy their signature Peking Duck in elegant red-carpeted surrounds, but reserve well in advance or risk missing out.

🚇 F5 ✉ 17 Market Lane ☎ 9662 3655
🕐 Mon–Sat noon–3pm, 6–11pm, Sun 6–10.30pm 🚊 City Circle Tram

BAR LOURINHA ($$)

barlourinha.com.au

Vintage thermometers and other bric-a-brac above the bar greet you as you enter this warm and homey Spanish and Portuguese tapas bar. Try their legendary yellowtail kingfish.

🚇 F5 ✉ 37 Little Collins Street ☎ 9663 7890 🕐 Mon–Thu noon–11pm, Fri & Sat noon–1am 🚊 Tram 11, 12, 109

CITY WINE SHOP ($$)

citywineshop.net.au

Let the wine connoisseurs choose your bottle of wine from the store while you sit down at their little curb-side café-bar to enjoy small plates off the ever-changing blackboard menu. Or simply

HIGHER GROUND ($$)

highergroundmelbourne.com.au

A powerhouse of a café over three levels, dishing up breakfast, lunch and dinner under soaring ceilings. Grab a mezzanine nook or sit beneath glorious

arched windows to enjoy specialty coffee and an inventive breakfast made with local produce.

⊞ C6 ✉ 650 Little Bourke Street ☎ 8899 6219 🕐 Mon–Wed 7–4, Thu & Fri 7am–11pm, Sat 8am–11pm, Sun 8–4 🚉 Southern Cross 🚋 Tram 86, 96

HWARO KOREAN BBQ ($$)
hwaro.com.au

Enjoy authentic Korean food using high-quality meats which is cooked at your table on mini charcoal barbecues. Or order a huge, steaming bowl of *bibimbap* and tuck in.

⊞ C6 ✉ 562 Little Bourke Street ☎ 9642 5696 🕐 Daily 5.30–10pm 🚋 Tram 86, 96

IZAKAYA DEN ($$$)
izakayaden.com.au

Find the doorway and make your way downstairs to Izakaya Den's intriguing basement restaurant. Sit front row at the bar and watch the chefs cook your food. Then, wash it down with *umeshu*.

⊞ F5 ✉ Basement, 114 Russell Street ☎ 9654 2977 🕐 Mon–Fri noon–2.30, 5.30 till late, Sat 5.30pm till late 🚋 Tram 86, 96

MAMASITA ($$)
mamasita.com.au

Melbourne is all over Mexican food, and Mamasita is where patrons patiently queue on the stairwell to get into this top-notch taqueria. A good choice of tacos and tostadas await to satisfy both the veggie and meat eater.

⊞ G5 ✉ Level 1, 11 Collins Street ☎ 9650 3821 🕐 Mon–Thu 5–10pm, Fri noon–11, Sat 5–11pm, Sun 5–10pm 🚋 City Circle Tram

MIZNON ($)
miznonaustralia.com

A fun and energetic atmosphere awaits when you pull up a bar stool and explore Mediterranean street food in the shape of a pita. Raise a glass to celebrity chef Eyal Shani, and to the signature whole-served roasted cauliflower.

⊞ D5 ✉ 59 Hardware Lane ☎ 9670 2861 🕐 Mon–Fri noon–11pm, Sat 10.30am–11pm 🚋 Tram 19, 57, 59

MOVIDA AQUI ($$)
movida.com.au

One of four Melbourne MoVida restaurants, this one serves up exquisite tapas in an airy terrace restaurant with cityscape views. Run by chef Frank Camorra, the big space has a big menu to match, but staff are on hand to guide you through it.

⊞ D6 ✉ Level 1, 500 Bourke Street ☎ 9663 3038 🕐 Mon–Fri noon–late, Sat 6pm–late 🚋 Tram 86, 96

PELLEGRINI'S ESPRESSO BAR ($)

A Melbourne institution since the 1950s, Pellegrini's is a classic Italian coffee bar/diner offering excellent espresso and colossal helpings of minestrone, pastas and salads. You can't beat the spaghetti bolognese, but it just might beat you.

⊞ F5 ✉ 66 Bourke Street ☎ 9662 1885 🕐 Breakfast, lunch and dinner daily 🚋 Tram 85, 96

ROSA'S CANTEEN ($$)
rosascanteen.com.au

Sit beneath huge windows that look out across the treetops and enjoy seasonal Sicilian food served with warmth. If you can't make a decision between the fettucine with duck and porcini ragu or the ravioli with oxtail ragu, then be sure to ask Rosa.

⊞ D6 ✉ Corner of Little Bourke & Thomson streets ☎ 9602 5491 🕐 Mon–Fri 12.30–3pm & 5–10pm, Sat 5.30–10pm 🚋 Tram 86, 96

Around Flinders Street

Centered on the dramatic Federation Square and accessible by the free City Circle Tram, the area around Flinders Street has some of Melbourne's top attractions and pleasant riverside walks.

Top 25

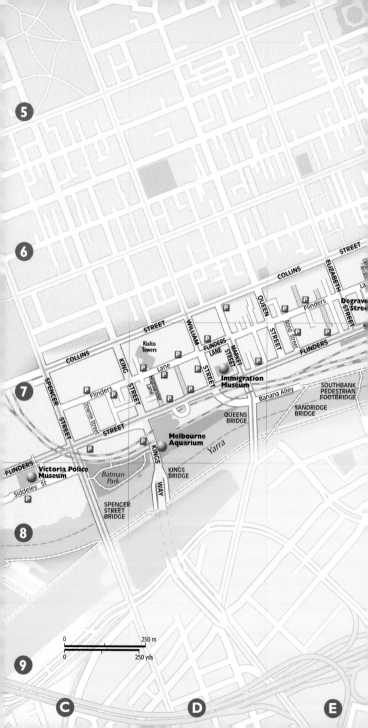

5

6

STREET

COLLINS

ELIZABETH
STREET

La

Flinders

Degrave
Stree

Queen

STREET

Bond Street

Rialto
Towers

STREET

WILLIAM

FLINDERS
LANE

MARKET
STREET

FLINDERS

STREET

COLLINS

KING

Lane

Highlander
Lane

STREET

Immigration
Museum

Banana Alley

SOUTHBANK
PEDESTRIAN
FOOTBRIDGE

7

SPENCER

Flinders

Downie Street

STREET

QUEENS
BRIDGE

SANDRIDGE
BRIDGE

STREET

STREET

KINGS

Melbourne
Aquarium

Yarra

FLINDERS

Victoria Police
Museum

Siddeley St

Batman
Park

KINGS
BRIDGE

KINGS

WAY

SPENCER
STREET
BRIDGE

8

0   250 m

0   250 yds

9

C   **D**   **E**

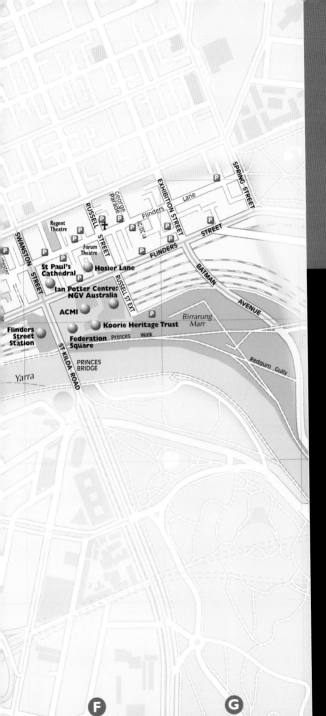

Regent
Theatre

George
Parade

RUSSELL
STREET

SWANSTON
STREET

Flinders
Lane

Lane

SPRING STREET

EXHIBITION STREET

FLINDERS

STREET

Forum
Theatre

St Paul's
Cathedral

Hosier Lane

Ian Potter Centre:
NGV Australia

ACMI

RUSSELL ST EXT

BATMAN

AVENUE

Koorie Heritage Trust

Birrarung
Marr

Flinders
Street
Station

Federation
Square

Princes

Walk

Redgum Gully

ST KILDA ROAD

PRINCES
BRIDGE

Yarra

F

G

Federation Square

HIGHLIGHTS

- Ian Potter Centre: NGV Australia
- ACMI
- Guided tours
- Free concerts at Deakin Edge
- Birrarung Marr

TIP

- Guided tours of Fed Square take place Monday to Saturday at 11am.

Federation Square is a cultural precinct and public square billed as Melbourne's meeting place, with top attractions including the Ian Potter Centre, ACMI and a host of restaurants, cafés and bars.

What's on? There's always something interesting happening in this huge complex, which covers a full city block. Built over an old railway yard, Fed Square (as it is known locally) was conceived as a civic heart for the city, and has enough museums, galleries, free attractions and places to dine to keep you busy for at least a day. It has its own "Fed TV" where you can pull up a deckchair and enjoy sporting and artistic content. The Deakin Edge, a 450-seat indoor amphitheater, often stages free theater, comedy, talks and presentations, and cabaret.

Clockwise from far left: The futuristic Federation Square is dominated by high-rise office buildings; the square is a popular gathering place for students; there's no shortage of watering holes in the square; the fragmented designs of the cultural buildings are reflected on the inside

Cultural square While the prime attraction is the excellent Ian Potter Centre: NGV Australia (▷ 46), with its superb collections, the state-of-the-art, high-tech galleries, cinemas and studio spaces of the Australian Centre for the Moving Image (ACMI, ▷ 49) will give you the lowdown on everything from more than a century of film history to the history of computer games and the latest digital art.

Green spaces The adjacent Birrarung Marr park lies on the north bank of the Yarra River and provides a link between the CBD and Melbourne's main sporting precinct. This contemporary park is part of a continuous green belt of parkland around the city. Festivals and events are held here along the river. The park also has a big children's playground.

THE BASICS
fedsquare.com
➕ F7
✉ Corner of Flinders and Swanston streets
☎ 9655 1900
🕐 Various times for museums
🍴 Restaurants and bars
🚇 Flinders Street
🚊 City Circle Tram
♿ Good
💷 Public areas free; admission to attractions
❓ Free tours Mon–Sat at 11am

Hosier Lane

HIGHLIGHTS

● Ever-changing street and graffiti art
● Rutledge Lane
● MoVida
● Bar Tini

TIP

● Get there early to beat the ever-increasing crowds of people taking selfies with amazing graffiti backdrops.

The ever-changing streetscape of graffiti-covered Hosier Lane famously featured a Banksy rat that got cleaned up by a council worker, and now plays host to talented local artists like Adnate and his huge mural of an Aboriginal boy.

History of Hosier Started up in the 1990s by artist Andy Mac, who had a gallery here, Hosier Lane has become Melbourne's controversial center for graffiti and street art featuring artists like Melbourne's Reka and Brisbane's Anthony Lister. Mac moved out in 2010, the Banksy rat got sanitized, taggers took over and it was up in the air what might happen to the laneway.

Melbourne Now In 2013, the National Gallery of Victoria came to the rescue with the

The most photographed laneway in Melbourne

"Melbourne Now" exhibition featuring "All Your Walls." Hosier Lane became a blank canvas and over 100 street artists gave the lane new murals, paste-ups and stencils. The year 2013 also saw local artist Adrian Doyle's *Empty Nursery Blue* make a statement on Rutledge Lane, off Hosier. His blue walls lasted less than an hour before fresh art popped up. Today you can't move for people taking photographs and sometimes you can't see past all the tagging, but where else does street art like Melbourne—self-proclaimed street-art capital of the world?

Street art tours Get the inside info from Melbourne Street Tours (melbournestreettours.com) with artist-guides like Ruskidd, who featured in the NGV's "Melbourne Now," and David Russel, a leading street art photographer.

THE BASICS
✚ F6
✉ Hosier Lane
🍴 MoVida, MoVida Next Door, Bar Tini
🚆 Flinders Street
🚋 City Circle Tram
🚹 Moderate
❓ Melbourne Street Tours (☎ 9328 5556) take you to Hosier Lane and to some of the lesser-known public art laneways.

Ian Potter Centre: NGV Australia

TOP 25

The interior space of this superb gallery is almost as good as the collection itself

This stunning venue contains the world's largest collection of Australian art, on display in 20 galleries over three levels. Major traditional and contemporary Indigenous works are presented alongside non-Indigenous art.

Indigenous art The Ian Potter Centre houses an Aboriginal and Torres Strait Islander collection of great depth and complexity. There are more than 3,000 works on display, including William Barak's *Figures in Possum Skin Cloaks* (1898), Emily Kngwarreye's *Big Yam Dreaming* (1995) and works by Ginger Riley, Lin Onus and Julie Gough.

Australian Impressionism Paintings by the Heidelberg School artists such as Arthur Streeton's *The Purple Noon's Transparent Might* (1896), Tom Roberts' *Shearing the Rams* (1890) and Frederick McCubbin's triptych *The Pioneer* (1904) are featured alongside the work of Jane Sutherland.

Exhibitions What you see on display barely touches the surface of the NGV's entire collection. Temporary and permanent exhibitions cover the gamut from paintings and sculpture to decorative arts. You might catch *Evening Coming in on Sydney Harbour* (1975) by Brett Whiteley and Sidney Nolan's *Footballer* (1946) as well as works by Margaret Preston, Arthur Boyd, John Brack and Fred Williams. Lina Bryans' *The Babe is Wise* (1940) may also be viewable.

On board ship at the
Immigration Museum
(left); displays at the
museum (right)

Immigration Museum

Head to the Old Customs House to learn about the strength and determination of immigrants who now call Australia home. Voices, images, letters and artifacts bring Victoria's immigration history to life.

Hardships revisited In this innovative museum special exhibitions sensitively explore themes of departure and arrival, journeys and settlement, and document the effects of immigration in Victoria since the early 1800s. Here you can walk through the re-creation of several ships' cabins and experience the cramped quarters endured by immigrants from the 1850s onward on their way to Victoria. The Immigration Discovery Centre has a library that focuses on cultural heritage and immigration, where you can look up information on family history. Outside, at the rear of the museum, is the Tribute Garden, a memorial courtyard bearing the names of immigrants. It's worth a visit for the building alone. The centerpiece of the museum is the elegant Long Room, a marvelous piece of Renaissance Revival architecture, featuring 16 columns and a mosaic tile floor.

Community festivals A few times a year the museum's courtyard plays host to community festivals, showcasing the food, music and culture of people from around the world. Themed festivals take place too, and past festivals have included an Islamic Arts Festival, a Sweets Festival and even a "Melt Chocolate" Festival, which, of course, featured Belgian immigrants.

THE BASICS

museumsvictoria.com.au/
immigrationmuseum
+ D7
✉ 400 Flinders Street
☎ 13 11 02
🕐 Daily 10–5
🍴 Café
🚉 Southern Cross or
Flinders Street
🚋 City Circle Tram
♿ Good
💲 Inexpensive
❓ Visitor guides are available in English, Chinese, French, German, Italian and Japanese. There's a daily tour at 2.30pm.

HIGHLIGHTS

● "Ship" experience
● The Long Room
● Tribute Garden
● Immigration Discovery Centre

TIP

● The Immigration Museum is autism friendly and has a map of low- and high-sensory spaces.

SEA LIFE Melbourne Aquarium

The waterside setting (left); the fascinating oceanarium (right)

THE BASICS

melbourneaquarium.com.au

➕ D7

✉ Corner of Flinders and King streets

☎ 9620 0999

🕐 Mon–Fri 10–5.30, Sat–Sun 9.30–6

🍴 Adventurer's Café, Croc Café

🚉 Southern Cross or Flinders Street

🚋 City Circle Tram

♿ Very good

💲 Expensive

❓ Glass-bottom boat tours, lots of talks and feeding sessions

HIGHLIGHTS

● Diving with the sharks
● Pinjarra, the saltwater crocodile
● Ice Age 4-D cinema
● Discovery Rockpools
● Deep-sea trench
● Themed retail outlet
● Walk-through tunnels

TIPS

● School holidays and weekends can be busy.
● Reserve online and save 20 percent.

Take an exhilarating underwater journey that gets you up close to sharks, rays, crocodiles, penguins and a multitude of other marine creatures.

Discovery zones For a touch and feel experience, the Discovery Rockpools let you get up close to starfish (or sea stars as the experts call them), hermit crabs and sea cucumbers, and watch baby fish play in the mangroves. Find Nemo the clownfish in the Coral Caves and crawl through the Bay of Rays display where you're likely to see a sawfish and a smooth stingray. Over at Seahorse Pier spot seahorses and cuttlefish, and learn about the Weedy Seadragon breeding program. There's even a Rainforest Adventure filled with snakes, frogs and turtles. Fuel up at the Adventurer's Café.

The Mermaid Garden For an insight into the diverse inhabitants of the Great Southern Ocean, walk down to the 2.2 million liter oceanarium, beneath the ground floor. Here you can walk along see-through tunnels, surrounded by a diverse array of sharks and rays, and myriad multicolored fish.

Action stations For an even more exhilarating experience, walk through the Crocodile Lair and see Pinjarra, a monster saltwater crocodile. Or dive with sharks, if you dare. Slightly more sedate, but also exhilarating, are the King and Gentoo penguins splashing about in the Penguin Playground.

ACMI

acmi.net.au

At the Australian Centre for the Moving Image, learn all you need to know about film and TV, video games and digital art. The center's permanent exhibition "Screen Worlds" has many interactive exhibits where you can bust a move on-screen, and put yourself right into the bullet scene from *The Matrix*.

🔢 F6 ✉ Federation Square ☎ 8663 2200 🕐 Daily 10–5 🚊 City Circle Tram ⚐ Very good 🎫 Free

DEGRAVES STREET

A bluestone cobbled laneway running between Flinders Street and Flinders Lane, Degraves is packed with café, bar and restaurant alfresco dining. A pink-tiled subway connects Degraves to Flinders Street Station. Boutique shops and art in glass cases line the walls of the subway.

🔢 E6 ✉ Degraves Street 🚊 City Circle Tram

FLINDERS STREET STATION

A wonder of French Renaissance architecture, Flinders Street Station was completed in 1909 and has since become a Melbourne icon. The steps under the dome's clocks are a famous meeting place for locals. The eye-catching yellow station is the busiest in Melbourne. The area around the station is a highlight of the White Night festival as buildings are lit up with incredible projections.

🔢 F7 ✉ Flinders Street ☎ 9610 7476 🕐 Daily 🚊 Flinders Street 🚊 City Circle Tram 🎫 Moderate

KOORIE HERITAGE TRUST

koorieheritagetrust.com

The trust's Cultural Centre features works by contemporary Aboriginal artists, plus a permanent exhibition that includes traditional artifacts and rare books. Its oral history unit offers a fascinating insight into the rich history and culture of Australia's southeastern Indigenous people. Sign up for a program or workshop to learn about Aboriginal culture and history.

🔢 F7 ✉ The Yarra Building, Federation Square ☎ 8622 6300 🕐 Daily 10–5 🚊 City Circle Tram 🎫 Free

ST. PAUL'S CATHEDRAL

stpaulscathedral.org.au

With its lofty spires and towers, beautiful stonework and magnificent stained glass, this Anglican cathedral is a classic example of Gothic revival architecture from the late 19th century. Inside you will see carved cedar woodwork, tiled floors and detailed stonework.

🔢 F6 ✉ Corner of Swanston and Flinders streets ☎ 9653 4220 🕐 Mon–Fri 8.30–6, Sat 9–4, Sun 7.30–7.30 🚊 City Circle Tram 🎫 Free

VICTORIA POLICE MUSEUM

policemuseum.vic.gov.au

This museum preserves old police records, photographs and artifacts from the 1800s. Among the crime paraphernalia of mugshots, weapons and photographs, find a couple of sets of original Ned Kelly Gang armor.

🔢 C8 ✉ Mezzanine level, 637 Flinders Street ☎ 9247 5214 🕐 Mon–Fri 10–4 🚊 Flinders Street 🚊 City Circle Tram 🎫 Donation

Shopping

THE CATS MEOW

thecatsmeow.com.au

If you're looking for original women's clothing head to The Cats Meow. It's an independent clothing store stocking only Australian designers—creations are quirky and colorful, and are made to fit women of all shapes and sizes.

✚ E6 ✉ Shop 9, Campbell Arcade, Degraves Street ☎ 9654 3011 🕐 Mon–Fri 10.30–6.30, Sat 10.30–5 🚋 City Circle Tram

CITY BASEMENT BOOKS

citybasementbooks.com.au

Quality secondhand books of every genre, topic and description. With so many books to choose from, helpful staff and great prices, it's guaranteed you'll leave with a bagful of books.

✚ E7 ✉ 342 Flinders Street ☎ 9620 0428 🕐 Mon–Fri 10–6, Sat 10–2 🚋 City Circle Tram

CITY HATTERS

cityhatters.com.au

Since 1910, City Hatters have been fitting hats to the heads of governor generals, actors and the public. Drop into the store under the Flinders Street Station clocks and pick up an Australian bush Akubra Coolabah hat for maximum sun protection.

✚ E7 ✉ 211 Flinders Street ☎ 9614 3294 🕐 Mon–Fri 9.30–6, Sat 9–5, Sun 10–4 🚋 City Circle Tram

CRAFT VICTORIA

craft.org.au

Beautiful, calm retail and exhibition spaces feature contemporary Australian craft and design. Come to view or buy jewelry, ceramics, glassware and textiles.

✚ F6 ✉ Watson Place ☎ 9650 7775 🕐 Mon–Wed 11–6, Thu–Fri 11–7, Sat 10–5 🚋 City Circle Tram

CRUMPLER

crumpler.com

Starting out in Melbourne back in the 1990s, Crumpler now makes bags for customers around the world. Pick up a lightweight duffle bag to bring back all those gifts you plan to take home.

✚ E6 ✉ 40–44 Degraves Street ☎ 9639 2954 🕐 Mon–Fri 8.30–6.30, Sat & Sun 10–6 🚋 City Circle Tram

IL PAPIRO

ilpapirofirenze.com.au

Step back in time to when thoughts were jotted down using ink and paper. This beautiful shop is chock full of top-quality Italian journals for you to write about your travels. Lovely wallet selection, too.

✚ E6 ✉ Shop 5, Degraves Street ☎ 9654 0955 🕐 Mon 10–5.30, Tue–Fri 10–6, Sat 10–5 🚋 City Circle Tram

RETROSTAR VINTAGE CLOTHING

retrostar.com.au

Retrostar has the largest vintage clothing array in Australia, specializing in the 1940s to 90s and covering a serious amount of clothes as well as bags, shoes and sunnies. Guaranteed to find that vintage T here.

✚ F6 ✉ 1/37 Swanston Street ☎ 9663 1223 🕐 Mon–Thu & Sat 10–6, Fri 10–7, Sun 11–5 🚋 City Circle Tram

SUGAR STATION

sugarstation.com.au

One for the little (and big) kids, this place is choc full of sweets, lollies, jelly beans, chocolates and sodas. Danger: it's self service. You'll be buzzing around Melbourne in no time!

✚ E6 ✉ 60 Elizabeth Street ☎ 9939 8751 🕐 Mon–Thu 8am–10pm, Fri 8am–midnight, Sat 10am–midnight, Sun 10–9 🚋 Tram 11, 12, 109

Entertainment and Nightlife

ARBORY BAR & EATERY

arbory.com.au

Outdoor Arbory runs for over 100 meters along the banks of the Yarra. It does some fabulous and affordable cocktails, all-day sandwiches and burgers, and heaps of share plates.

⊞ E7 ✉ Flinders Walk ☎ 8648 7644 🕐 Daily 7.30am–late 🚋 City Circle Tram

BAR TINI

bartini.com.au

For cocktails, wine and sherry head to Bar Tini. A hidden Spanish bodega, it's part of the MoVida mob so enjoy fabulous tapas, too.

⊞ F6 ✉ 3–5 Hosier Lane ☎ 9663 3038 🕐 Tue–Sat 5pm–late 🚋 City Circle Tram

BEER DELUXE

beerdeluxe.com.au

Burger bar up top on the Federation Square concourse and bar and beer garden down below. There's always a world-class brew on tap or in the fridge.

⊞ F6 ✉ Federation Square ☎ 9810 0093 🕐 Daily 11.30am–late 🚋 City Circle Tram

CHERRY BAR

cherrybar.com.au

Cherry Bar is an authentic rock 'n' roll bar, with local and international acts taking to the tiny stage, as well as DJs spinning vinyl into the wee hours.

⊞ F6 ✉ 103 Flinders Lane ☎ 9639 8122 🕐 Mon–Wed 5pm–3am, Thu–Sat 5pm–5am, Sun 2pm–3am 🚋 City Circle Tram

EAU DE VIE

eaudevie.com.au

Once you've found this hidden bar you'll be transported to 1920s prohibition America. Grab a booth in this speakeasy or go behind the bookcase for a dram in the Whisky Room.

⊞ F6 ✉ 1 Malthouse Lane ☎ 8393 9367 🕐 Mon–Thu 5pm–1am, Fri & Sat 4pm–1am, Sun 4pm–11pm 🚋 City Circle Tram

THE FORUM

forummelbourne.com.au

The interior of the Forum will distract you with its marble staircases, star-sky ceiling and Romanesque theater stage until some of the world's best bands blow you away or the Comedy Festival has you rolling on the floor.

⊞ F6 ✉ Corner of Flinders and Russell streets ☎ 9299 9990 🚋 City Circle Tram

RIVERLAND BAR

riverlandbar.com

Riverland offers stunning river views, a great wine list, a variety of draft beers from around the world, as well as a decent menu.

⊞ F7 ✉ Vaults 1–9, Federation Wharf ☎ 9662 1771 🕐 Daily 11am–late 🚋 City Circle Tram

TRANSPORT HOTEL

transporthotel.com.au

Huge bar with three beer gardens overlooking the Yarra River and Fed Square. Lots of shared plates, pizzas and burgers to keep hunger at bay. Head upstairs to Taxi Kitchen for Southeast-Asian cuisine.

⊞ F7 ✉ Corner of Princes Bridge and Northbank ☎ 9654 8808 🕐 Daily 11am–late 🚆 Flinders Street

YOUNG AND JACKSONS

youngandjacksons.com.au

Melbourne's most famous pub is the location of *Chloe*, a nude painting that shocked the city in the late 19th century. Find her in the a la carte dining area upstairs.

⊞ F6 ✉ 1 Swanston Street ☎ 9650 3884 🕐 Daily 10am–late 🚋 City Circle Tram

Where to Eat

PRICES

Prices are approximate, based on a
3-course meal for one person.

$	A$25–A$45
$$	A$46–A$75
$$$	A$76–A$120

BRUNETTI ($)

brunetti.com.au

Brunetti's Italian-style coffee and cakes
in the patisserie, and pizza and pasta in
the *paninoteca* have got you covered
for the day, with a gelato bar and a
Campari bar too.

➕ A6 ✉ 250 Flinders Lane ☎ 9347 2801
🕐 Sun–Thu 6am–11pm, Fri & Sat 6am–
midnight 🚋 City Circle Tram

CODA BAR & RESTAURANT ($$$)

codarestaurant.com.au

This stylish basement restaurant plates
chef Adam D'Sylva's contemporary, seasonal innovations. It's best to reserve
ahead, but walk-ins can sit at the bar.

➕ F6 ✉ 141 Flinders Lane ☎ 9650 3155
🕐 Daily noon–3, 6pm–late 🚋 City Circle Tram

CUMULUS INC ($$$)

cumulusinc.com.au

Acclaimed chef Andrew McConnell
serves breakfast, lunch and dinner at
this large bar-restaurant. Upstairs is the
equally delightful wine bar, Cumulus Up.

➕ G6 ✉ 45 Flinders Lane ☎ 9650 1445
🕐 Mon–Fri 7am–11pm, Sat–Sun 8am–11pm
🚋 City Circle Tram

HELLA GOOD ($)

hellagood.com.au

Brought to you by Melbourne's longest-
running Greek restaurant Stalactites, this
tiny takeaway joint serves up veggie,
chicken and lamb souvlaki, as well as
chips, dips and desserts.

➕ E6 ✉ 7 Elizabeth Street ☎ 9629 8239
🕐 Sun–Wed 11am–midnight, Thu 11am–3am,
Fri & Sat 11am–5am 🚋 City Circle Tram

KENZAN ($$)

kenzan.com.au

Here since 1981, Kenzan serves exceptional sushi and sashimi in a spacious
restaurant with sushi bar and private
dining nooks. Traditional Japanese fare
and excellent service.

➕ G6 ✉ 45 Collins Street ☎ 9654 8933
🕐 Mon–Fri noon–2.30 & 6pm–late, Sat 6pm–
late 🚋 City Circle Tram

KISUMÉ JAPANESE ($$)

kisume.com.au

Kisumé offers a superb sushi bar, restaurant, Chablis bar and private dining
rooms. Drop in for *otsumami*, where
you can choose a flight of saké or
whiskey, matched with beautifully
presented Japanese snacks.

➕ F6 ✉ 175 Flinders Lane ☎ 9671 4444
🕐 Daily noon–late 🚋 City Circle Tram

TRAMCAR RESTAURANT

One of Melbourne's dining institutions,
the burgundy Colonial Tramcar Restaurant
has been plying the streets of Melbourne
for more than 30 years. The first traveling
tramcar restaurant in the world, it carries
36 diners per tram and has a set charge
which includes three courses, cheeses and
Australian wines. Dishes are predominantly
Modern Australian cuisine. Be sure to make
reservations well ahead as it's very popular.
Dietary requirements must be advised no
later than 24 hours in advance.

➕ D8 ✉ Departs from Tram Stop 125
Normanby Road, near corner of Clarendon
Street (near Crown Casino) ☎ 9695 4000,
tramrestaurant.com.au 🕐 Lunch and
dinner daily

South of the Yarra

Across the Princes Bridge over the Yarra River are the leafy Royal Botanic Gardens, fashionable suburbs, the entertainment precinct of Southbank, which includes the Arts Centre, Southgate and Crown Casino, and South Wharf.

Top 25

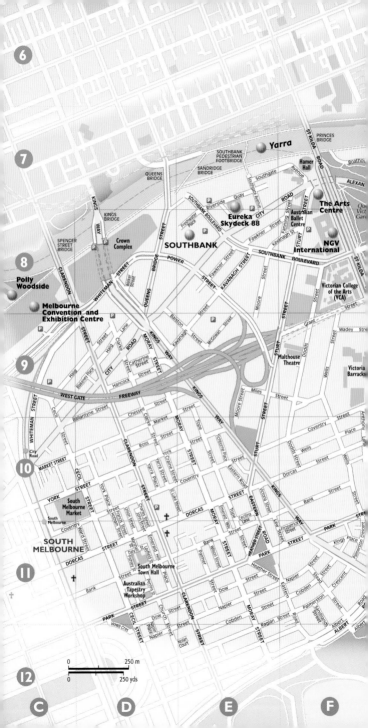

6

7

Yarra

SOUTHBANK PEDESTRIAN FOOTBRIDGE
SANDRIDGE BRIDGE
QUEENS BRIDGE

Southgate

Hamer Hall

PRINCES BRIDGE

ST KILDA ROAD

Boathou

ALEXAN

KINGS WAY

KINGS BRIDGE

SPENCER STREET BRIDGE

CLARENDON STREET

Riverside

Quay

Eureka Skydeck 88

SOUTHBANK

Freshwater Place

CITY ROAD

Avenue

Fawkner street

Fanning St

ROAD

Kavanagh St

Australian Ballet Centre

The Arts Centre

Que Vict Gate

NGV International

STURT STREET

Crown Complex

Water Street

P

BRIDGE STREET

POWER STREET

QUEENS STREET

Fawkner street

SOUTHBANK BOULEVARD

ST KILDA ROAD

8
Polly Woodside

Melbourne Convention and Exhibition Centre

Ballston street

Kavanagh

McGowan street

KAVANAGH STREET

Moore street

Grant

Victorian College of the Arts (VCA)

street

Wadey Stree

CLARENDON STREET

P

Halls Lane

Clarke Street

MORAY STREET

KINGS WAY

Catherine Street

Hancock street

CITY ROAD

street

P

Malthouse Theatre

Dodds

Wells

Miles street

STURT STREET

Victoria Barracks

9

WEST GATE FREEWAY

WHITEMAN STREET

Cecil street

Ballantyne street

Chessell street

Clare street

Market street

Ross street

York Place

Tope street

KINGS WAY

street

Eastern Road

Coventry

Wells

Anthony Lane

Place

10

City Road

MARKET STREET

CECIL STREET

York Place

York Crane Street

Yarra Place

Coventry

CLARENDON STREET

MORAY STREET

Emerald Way

Eastern Place

DORCAS STREET

EASTERN ROAD

Cecilia Lane

Emma street

KINGS WAY

Bank

Dorcas

Wells

YORK STREET

South Melbourne Market

South Melbourne

St Vincent Place South

Dundas Place

St Vincent Place North

Emerald Hill Place

DORCAS STREET

Bank

Palmer street

Emerald Way

Milton street

PARK STREET

Kings Place

Park

SOUTH MELBOURNE

Coventry

Ward Street

STREET

DORCAS

Emerald Hill Place

David St

South Melbourne Town Hall

Australian Tapestry Workshop

Bank

CLARENDON STREET

Palmer street

Milton street

Heather street

HEATHER STREET

Napier

PARK STREET

Cobden

MORAY STREET

Napier

Palmerston

Albert

11

Bank

PARK

CECIL STREET

Howe Cres

Crown street

Church Street

Nolan Court

Napier

CLARENDON STREET

Cobden

Raglan street

MORAY STREET

Albert

EASTERN ROAD

Crescent

Kings Place

Palmerston

Road

Albert

12

0   250 m
0   250 yds

C   **D**   **E**   **F**

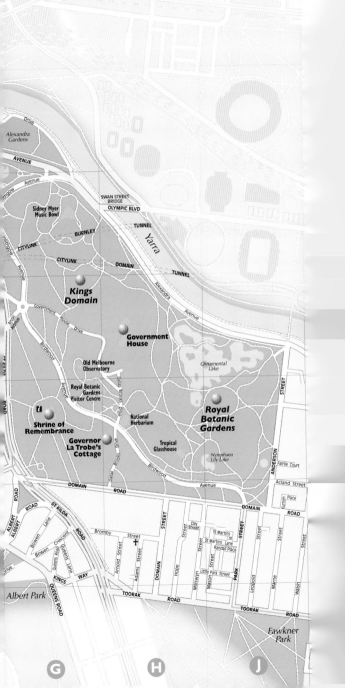

The Arts Centre

Dominated by its elegant spire, the Arts Centre complex sits proudly by the river

THE BASICS

artscentremelbourne.
com.au

✚ F7

✉ 100 St. Kilda Road

☎ Information: 9281 8000.
Ticketing: 1300 182 183

🕐 Mon–Fri 6am–late, Sat 8.30am–late, Sun 10–5 or after last performance

🍴 Cafés and bars

🚋 Tram 1, 3, 5, 6, 16, 64, 67, 72

♿ Excellent

👋 Moderate

❓ Guided tours Mon–Sat 11am inc morning tea. Backstage tour Sun 11am

HIGHLIGHTS

● Elegant spire
● Yarra River location
● Concert Hall
● Artworks
● Theatres Building
● Performing Arts Museum
● Guided tours

The city's bastion of high culture is dominated by the spire of the Theatres Building. The Hamer Hall, the State Theatre, the Playhouse and the Fairfax Studio are all found here.

Hamer Hall This circular building next to the Yarra River is the city's main performing arts venue and home of the Melbourne Symphony Orchestra and the Australian Chamber Orchestra. The hall features a lavish interior, and a large collection of Australian art, and draws performers from around the world.

Theatres Building Linked to Hamer Hall by a walkway, this building houses the Playhouse, the State Theatre and the Fairfax Studio. The State Theatre is home to the Australian Ballet and Opera Australia. Overlooking the Yarra, next to Saké Restaurant, is The Channel, a community arts learning lab. Interesting and changing exhibitions of theater costumes, set designs and other memorabilia are held in the Centre foyers. Gallery 1, the major exhibition space, adjacent to the St. Kilda Road entrance, has exhibitions that complement The Arts Centre's performance program. The Playhouse Theatre foyers house a collection of Western Desert paintings by important Indigenous artists.

Sidney Myer Music Bowl This popular, outdoor summer venue, set in the nearby Kings Domain gardens (▷ 63), hosts everything from rock concerts to opera soloists.

The huge Eureka Tower is topped by the Skydeck, for amazing views of the city

Eureka Skydeck 88

On the 88th level of the Eureka Tower, this observation deck includes a dramatic viewing experience in an extendable glass cube. It is Melbourne's tallest building at 297m (975ft).

What a view While waiting for the high-speed elevators to take you up, examine the 6m (20ft), multiuser, interactive Serendipity Table that explores the stories and history of Melbourne. Once on the Skydeck, you are presented with a variety of viewing options. Besides the multidirectional glassed-in viewing sectors, there's a caged zone, The Terrace, where you can brave the outside elements.

Close to The Edge An additional thrill is available if you choose to purchase a ticket for The Edge—a 3m square (10ft) glass cube that slides out from the building when it has its quota of brave souls on board. It's a weird sensation to be suspended almost 300m (980ft) above the ground. In poor weather conditions and high wind speeds, The Edge may not be operational. The Kiosk 88 serves drinks, snacks and ice creams; the gift shop has souvenirs and gifts.

Statistics Eureka Skydeck 88 was completed in 2006, taking four years to build, at a cost of around A$500 million. The 13 lifts, the fastest in the southern hemisphere, travel in excess of 9m (30ft) per second. The top of the building can flex up to 600mm (2ft) in high winds.

THE BASICS

eurekaskydeck.com.au

➕ E7

✉ Riverside Quay, Southbank

☎ 9693 8888

🕐 Daily 10–10

🍴 Kiosk

🚉 Flinders Street

♿ Good

💲 Skydeck: expensive. The Edge: moderate. For a little bit extra you can buy a ticket that allows you to visit twice in one day or twice over two days.

HIGHLIGHTS

- Serendipity Table
- The Edge
- The Terrace
- Fine views

TIP

- Forget The Edge if heights worry you.

NGV International

Australia's foremost art gallery has a vast selection of superb international art from Europe, Asia, America and Oceania. The collections of the NGV are regarded as the most comprehensive in Australia, and some works are world renowned.

International collection This much-loved local icon, designed by Sir Roy Grounds in the early 1960s, was once home to an extensive collection of Australian and international art, but the NGV International has now morphed into a gallery that features international art only. The gallery has more than 70,000 works of art, dating from 2,400BC to the present day, including pre-Columbian artifacts, Greek and Roman antiquities, and a fine collection of American paintings and sculpture. European Old Masters

Exterior and interior views of the NGV International, which contains one of the greatest collections of international art in the world

include Tiepolo, Rubens and Rembrandt, and there are also works by Rodin, Picasso, Monet and Henry Moore. Photography, prints, costumes, textiles and decorative arts from all periods are represented by exquisite examples, presented in elegant and dramatic surroundings. Particularly worth looking out for is the Leonard French stained-glass ceiling of the Great Hall, and the Asian art galleries.

Temporary exhibitions NGV International's diverse program of special exhibitions, in conjunction with national and international art museums, brings in the works of exceptional artists from around the world. The information desk has details of NGV Friday Nights, exhibitions, lectures, floor talks, tours, films and children's activities on offer from time to time.

THE BASICS

ngv.vic.gov.au
F8
180 St. Kilda Road
8620 2222
Daily 10–5
Restaurant and café
Tram 1, 3, 5, 6, 16, 64, 67, 72
Excellent
Free (charges for some exhibitions)
Free tours daily, lectures, films, library and design shop

Royal Botanic Gardens

HIGHLIGHTS

- Visitor center
- Plants in season
- Tree ferns
- Guided walks
- Ornamental lake
- Species names
- Riverside walk
- Jardin Tan kiosk and restaurant
- Punting on the lake

TIP

- The gardens are best visited in the early morning during the summer months.

Lush lawns and a labyrinth of forest walks await those who choose to escape the bustle of the city. Have a picnic under a tree, glide over the lake in a punt, or explore the plant collections.

The gardens Established by Lieutenant Governor Charles La Trobe in 1846, the botanic gardens have been a center for horticulture, science and conservation for more than 170 years. Botanists Ferdinand von Mueller (working here from 1857–73) and William Guilfoyle (working 1873–1909) created the rolling lawns, formal flower gardens, wooded coppices and lake you see today. More than 8,500 plant species from around the world are in all stages of bud and blossom at any given time. Fern Gully is a cool, tranquil spot beneath shady tree

Take a break from the busy city at the beautiful Royal Botanic Gardens

ferns and Guilfoyle's Volcano pops up out of the old reservoir giving magnificent views of the city. See palms in the Tropical Glasshouse, and a mind-boggling array of plants and fungi in the National Herbarium.

Observatory Gate This entrance to the gardens is the ideal orientation point for your visit. At the visitor center you can reserve a guided tour, browse the gardens, shop for unusual souvenirs, and enjoy a snack in the Jardin Tan café.

Aboriginal Heritage Walks On these walks, guides share their knowledge of the area and the life of the Kulin (Koolin) people, who lived in the Melbourne area before Europeans arrived. You'll learn about their use of local plants, their culture and their history.

THE BASICS

rbg.vic.gov.au

🔢 J10

✉ Birdwood Avenue

☎ 9252 2300. Aboriginal Heritage Walks: 9252 2429

🕐 Gardens: daily 7.30am–sunset

🍴 Jardin Tan and The Terrace

🚃 Tram 3, 5, 6, 16, 64, 67 and 72 (Stop 19 Shrine of Remembrance/St. Kilda Rd)

♿ Excellent

💲 Free

❓ Garden Discovery tours daily 10.30am and 2pm; Aboriginal Heritage Walks Sun–Fri at 11am

Southbank and the Yarra River

TOP 25

Take a stroll along the Yarra for the latest in entertainment, dining and nightlife

THE BASICS

➕ Southbank E8; Crown Complex D8; Cruises F7

✉ Crown Entertainment Complex, Southbank

☎ Crown Casino 9292 8888

🕐 Daily

🍴 Cafés and restaurants

🚉 Flinders Street

🚋 Southbank City Circle Tram; Crown Complex 12, 96, 109

♿ Moderate

💲 Free

❓ Boat tours on the Yarra: Melbourne River Cruises ☎ 8610 2600; City River Cruises ☎ 0450 778 000

HIGHLIGHTS

● River promenade
● Public art
● Shopping and eating
● Cinemas and clubs
● Casino
● View from the Princes Bridge
● River cruises
● Cycleways
● City lights at night

Melburnians come here in great numbers on weekends to stroll along the river, shop at boutiques, eat out and try their luck at the nearby Crown Casino.

Southbank This riverside district was once a dingy industrial area covered with warehouses and workshops. Now a popular spot for shopping and dining, many of the city's attractions are located here, alongside the Arts Centre and NGV International. Large sculptures line the riverbank and a footbridge joins Southbank's Southgate complex to the city. Look for the famous sculpture *Ophelia*, by Melbourne artist Deborah Halpern. In summer, the arts festival sees free performances along Southbank.

Yarra River Cruises The down-river cruise meanders past the city CBD and Southbank, along the historical Victoria Docks, and on to the Docklands area. An upstream trip will take you past lovely parks, gardens and stylish suburban architecture. The Royal Botanic Gardens, Herring Island and the Melbourne Cricket Ground are highlights (cityrivercruises.com.au).

Crown Complex A casino, cinemas, cafés, cabarets, bars, restaurants and nightclubs keep the Crown Entertainment Complex lively, especially on weekends. Along the promenade are monoliths that overflow with water by day and, when you least expect it, shoot fireballs at night. Gambling is taken seriously in Victoria. Get help at responsiblegambling.vic.gov.au.

CHAPEL STREET
Chapel Street is a fashionista, foodie and clubber's delight. Australian designer shops line the street from South Yarra to Prahran and Windsor, as well as a head-spinning amount of upmarket bars, clubs and restaurants.

➕ L13 on reverse of sheet map ✉ Chapel Street 🚋 Tram 78 ♿ Good

GOVERNMENT HOUSE
governor.vic.gov.au

Set in quiet gardens, this mansion was built in 1876 as the official residence of the Governor of Victoria. Inside is magnificently furnished, with a ballroom larger than that of London's Buckingham Palace.

➕ H9 ✉ Government House Drive ☎ National Trust Tours 9656 9889 🕐 Tours Mon, Thu 10am 🚋 Tram 3, 5, 6, 16, 64, 67, 72 ♿ Few 💲 Moderate

GOVERNOR LA TROBE'S COTTAGE
This pretty little cottage, Victoria's first Government House, was brought from England in 1839 by Charles La Trobe, who became the first Lieutenant-Governor of the young colony. First set up at Jolimont, the building was relocated and restored by Australia's National Trust, and many of the furnishings are original.

➕ H10 ✉ Birdwood Avenue ☎ 9656 9889 🕐 Oct–Apr Sun 2–4pm. Tours Mon & Thu 10am year round 🚋 Tram 3, 5, 6, 16, 64, 67, 72 ♿ Few 💲 Inexpensive

KINGS DOMAIN
A major urban green space, Kings Domain is home to the Sidney Myer Music Bowl, Governor La Trobe's Cottage (▷ left), and the impressive Shrine of Remembrance (▷ 64). The Alexandra Gardens and Queen Victoria Gardens adjoin the outstanding 36ha (89-acre) Royal Botanic Gardens (▷ 60–61), and together form a continuous park between Princes Bridge and South Yarra. A granite-boulder memorial in Linlithgow Avenue marks the remains of 38 Aboriginal

Governor La Trobe's cottage

people at Kings Domain Resting Place, repatriated from the Museum of Victoria in 1985.

🜨 G9 ✉ St. Kilda Road 🕐 Daily 🚊 Tram 3, 5, 6, 16, 64, 67, 72 ♿ Good 💲 Free

MELBOURNE CONVENTION & EXHIBITION CENTRE

mcec.com.au

Everything from talks to tours to expos takes place at the MCEC. Walk through the 6-star green-rated building, with its huge concourse, sloping roof and high glass facade, out onto South Wharf to enjoy restaurants and bars.

🜨 C8 ✉ 1 Convention Centre Place ☎ 9235 8000 🕐 Daily, depending on events 🚊 Tram 12, 96, 109 ♿ Excellent 💲 Free; fee for some events

POLLY WOODSIDE

nationaltrust.org.au/places/polly-woodside

Having circumnavigated the globe 17 times since 1885, there's no rest for this tall ship as she welcomes scallywags aboard to walk the plank and scrub the deck. A great day out

for kids, there's story times, and even the chance for budding pirates to yell a crew call. Virtual reality headsets are offered to those who are mobility impaired.

🜨 C8 ✉ 21 South Wharf Promenade ☎ 9656 9889 🕐 Sat–Sun 10–4 🚊 Tram 12, 96, 109 ♿ Few 💲 Moderate

SHRINE OF REMEMBRANCE

shrine.org.au

Melbourne's most recognized landmark, opened in 1934, is dedicated to those who died in World War I. It now honors all the men and women who have served Australia.

🜨 G10 ✉ Birdwood Avenue ☎ 9661 8100 🕐 Daily 10–5 🚊 Tram 3, 5, 6, 16, 64, 67, 72 ♿ Good 💲 Free

SOUTH YARRA AND PRAHRAN

One of the city's smartest areas, with designer clothing, antiques, fine art, and classy bars and restaurants.

🜨 L12/K14 on sheet map ✉ Toorak Road/Chapel Street 🍴 Many cafés, restaurants 🚊 Tram 58, 78

Polly Woodside

Shopping

CHAPEL STREET BAZAAR

facebook.com/chapelstreetbazaar

Packed to the gills with vintage clothing and collectibles, the Baz is where you might go for hard-to-find vinyl and books, but then end up leaving with a cute porcelain cat ornament or trinket.

🔳 Off L14 on sheet map 📧 217 Chapel St, Prahran VIC 3181 ☎ 9529 1727 🕐 Daily 10–6 🚊 Tram 78

DAKOTA 501

dakota501.com

For over 40 years this boutique denim retailer has specialized in quality local and international denim labels, including Levis, Lee, Diesel, Adidas and Autonomy.

🔳 Off L14 on sheet map 📧 245 Chapel Street, South Yarra ☎ 9529 5546 🕐 Mon–Sat 10–6, Sun 11–5 🚊 Tram 78

DINOSAUR DESIGNS

dinosaurdesigns.com.au

Striking colors and bold designs are prominent in the painted resin jewelry and homewares from Australia's top designers, Louise Olsen and Stephan Ormandy.

🔳 M12 on sheet map 📧 562 Chapel Street, South Yarra ☎ 9827 2600 🕐 Mon–Sat 10–6, Sun 11–5 🚊 Tram 78, 79

GREVILLE RECORDS

grevillerecords.com.au

Greville stocks a wide range of vinyl, plus books and paraphernalia. If you're still trying to find that rare Bob Dylan or Beatles record, it might well be here. For more than 30 years it has played host to in-store signings and live music.

🔳 Off L14 on sheet map 📧 152 Greville Street, Prahran ☎ 9510 3012 🕐 Mon–Thu 10–6, Fri 10–7, Sat 10–6, Sun 11–5 🚊 Tram 78

HAIGH'S CHOCOLATES

haighschocolates.com.au

The oldest family-owned chocolatier in Melbourne whips up bars, boxes and hampers of chocolates at this boutique store.

🔳 Off M12 on sheet map 📧 499 Toorak Road, South Yarra ☎ 9827 8713 🕐 Mon–Fri 9–6, Sat 9–5, Sun 11–5 🚊 Tram 58

JAM FACTORY

thejamfactory.com.au

Home to food outlets, a cinema and specialist shops, this former jam factory is a destination in its own right.

🔳 M13 on sheet map 📧 500 Chapel Street, South Yarra ☎ 9860 8500 🕐 Daily 9am–late 🚊 Tram 78

LE LOUVRE

lelouvre.com.au

Ever-changing fashion, art and design featuring international designer clothes by Gucci, Stella McCartney, Balmain and more. Its almost 100-year history of bringing fashion and art together sets it apart.

🔳 M12 on sheet map 📧 2 Daly Street, South Yarra ☎ 9650 1300 🕐 Mon–Fri 10–5.30, Sat 10–5 🚊 Tram 58, 78

NGV DESIGN STORE

store.ngv.vic.gov.au

Part exhibition merchandise, part local designer wares and part book shop, the NGV Design Store has almost too much

UPMARKET SHOPS

Shops at the upper end of Collins Street, and in South Yarra and Toorak, sell international designer labels. Other international shops include Burberry, Bvlgari and Prada at the Crown Entertainment Complex, (▷ 62) and the Galleria Plaza shops.

to look at after a few hours perusing the galleries. Pick up a postcard, shopping bag or hat, or head to the jewelry for an exclusive designer piece.

🟦 F8 ✉ 180 St. Kilda Road ☎ 8682 2243 🕐 Daily 10–5 🚋 Tram 1, 3, 5, 6, 16, 64, 67, 72

PRAHRAN MARKET

prahranmarket.com.au

This is where you go to stock up on all things ethical and organic, from free-range meats to sustainable seafood to all things deli. If you head there late you might get lucky and score a cheap bag of fruit or veg.

🟦 L14 on sheet map ✉ 163–185 Commercial Road ☎ 8290 8220 🕐 Tue–Sat 7–5, Sun 10–3 🚋 Tram 72, 78

SIMON JOHNSON: TOORAK

simonjohnson.com

This is where you'll find the perfect cheese platter and chocolates, for your super-extravagant picnic in the Royal Botanic Gardens. If you want to really indulge, caviar is the big thing here.

🟦 Off M12 on sheet map ✉ 471 Toorak Road 🕐 9644 3633 🕐 Mon–Fri 9–5.30, Sat 9–5, Sun 10–4 🚋 Tram 58

SOUTHGATE

southgatemelbourne.com.au

You could easily spend a day at this collection of eclectic shops, restaurants and bars just across the Yarra River from the city center. With three levels to explore, keep an eye out for the center's art collection that depicts Melbourne—seek out Loretta Quinn's *Crossing the First Threshold* sculpture that sits alone on a balcony.

🟦 E7 ✉ Southbank 🕐 9686 1000 🕐 Daily 10am–late 🚋 City Circle Tram

SOUTH MELBOURNE MARKET

southmelbournemarket.com.au

Everything from fresh fruit and vegetables to delicatessen items, great coffee and household goods.

🟦 C10 ✉ 322–326 Coventry Street, South Melbourne ☎ 9209 6295 🕐 Fri 8–5, Wed, Sat & Sun 8–4 🚈 South Melbourne 🚋 Tram 12, 96

SUNDAY ART MARKET

artscentremelbourne.com.au/your-visit/sunday-market

The Art Centre's lawn gets taken over every Sunday with stalls selling interesting and unusual hand-crafted works by local designers. There's also live music and plenty of stalls selling snacks.

🟦 F7 ✉ The Arts Centre 🕐 Sun 10–4 🚈 Flinders Street 🚋 Tram 1, 3, 5, 6, 16, 64, 67, 72

SYBER'S BOOKS

sybersbooks.com.au

Full of rare and out-of-print books, including Australian literature. Well-thumbed secondhand books abound here on 75 bulging bookcases.

🟦 Off L14 on sheet map ✉ 38 Chapel Street, South Yarra ☎ 9530 2222 🕐 Daily 11.30–5.30 🚈 Windsor 🚋 Tram 78

GEMS

Opals are the most popular gemstones sought out by visitors although you'll also find South Sea pearls, Argyle diamonds and original designs in Australian gold. Visit several shops to get an idea of the variety and price range before buying. Many shops have examples of rough stones and a few even have displays explaining the mining process. All are happy to answer questions.

Entertainment and Nightlife

BELLOTA WINE BAR

bellota.com.au

A wine bar housed in a classic Melbourne Victorian building, you're guaranteed a great selection as sister wine store, Prince Wine Store, is next door. Cheese and charcuterie are available to nibble on all day, or stay for dinner.

🔢 E11 ✉️ 181 Bank Street, South Melbourne ☎️ 9078 8381 🕐 Tue–Sat 11–11 🚋 Tram 1, 12, 96

HAMER HALL

artscentremelbourne.com.au

A stunning venue with superb acoustics, 2,500-seater Hamer Hall has seen jazz and rock greats grace the stage, as well as hosting performances by the Melbourne Symphony Orchestra and Australian Chamber Orchestra.

🔢 F7 ✉️ The Arts Centre, Southbank ☎️ 9281 8000 🕐 Daily 10–5.45, plus evening events 🚈 Flinders Street 🚋 Tram 1, 3, 5, 6, 16, 64, 67, 72

HOPSCOTCH

hopscotchmelbourne.com.au

Its own microbrewed beer makes up just a few of the 30 taps on offer here. Take a tasting paddle out to the beer garden with your bar snacks and burger; just leave room for the nitro ice-cream.

🔢 E7 ✉️ 2/4 Riverside Quay, Southbank ☎️ 9810 0099 🕐 Daily 11.30am–late 🚋 City Circle Tram

MALTHOUSE THEATRE

malthousetheatre.com.au

Inventive and thought-provoking performances at this innovative theater are sure to challenge expectations and start conversations—and where better to finish them than at the on-site Coopers Malthouse Bar?

🔢 A9 ✉️ 113 Sturt Street, Southbank ☎️ 9685 5111 🕐 Mon 9.30–5, Tue–Fri 9.30am–late, Sat 10.30am–late, Sun 5pm–late 🚋 Tram 1

MELBOURNE RECITAL CENTRE

melbournerecital.com.au

An architectural wonder with sensational acoustics. Showcases world-class music performances in the Elisabeth Murdoch Hall that's designed to look like the back of a rare and beautiful instrument.

🔢 F8 ✉️ 31 Sturt Street, Southbank ☎️ 9699 3333 🕐 Mon–Fri 9–5, plus evening events 🚋 Tram 1, 3, 5, 6, 16, 64, 67, 72

MELBOURNE SPORTS AND AQUATIC CENTRE

melbournesportshub.com.au/msac

A variety of swimming pools as well as a popular wave pool. Other sports include table tennis, basketball and volleyball.

🔢 Off map ✉️ Albert Park Road, Albert Park ☎️ 9926 1555 🕐 Mon–Fri 6am–10pm, Sat–Sun 7am–8pm 🚋 Tram 12, 96

PONYFISH ISLAND

ponyfish.com.au

Floating bar kiosk beneath the Yarra River footbridge. Descend from the Southgate Pedestrian Bridge for small bites, cocktails and fabulous sunsets.

🔢 E7 ✉️ Southbank Pedestrian Bridge 🕐 Daily 11am–late 🚋 City Circle Tram

STATE THEATRE

artscentremelbourne.com.au

Opera Australia and the Australian Ballet perform on one of the largest stages in the world here. And that's not all: come here to see dance and musicals, too.

🔢 F7 ✉️ The Arts Centre, Southbank ☎️ 9281 8000 🕐 Shows: daily 🚈 Flinders Street 🚋 Tram 1, 3, 5, 6, 16, 64, 67, 72

Where to Eat

PRICES
Prices are approximate, based on a 3-course meal for one person.
$ A$25–A$45
$$ A$46–A$75
$$$ A$76–A$120

eggs to Scotch eggs, plus a choice of buns with Wagyu burger, fried chicken and bacon slider—all with egg. A great spot for breakfast or lunch.

➕ D10 ✉ 303 Coventry Street, South Melbourne ☎ 99939 4239 🕐 Daily 7.30–3.30 🚋 Tram 96

ATLAS DINING ($$)

atlasdining.com.au

This restaurant is about travel, the cuisine changing every four months. Chef Charlie Carrington heads to each new country-of-origin to research, then plates up back in Melbourne.

➕ L14 on sheet map ✉ 133 Commercial Road, South Yarra ☎ 9826 2621 🕐 Tue–Fri 6pm–11pm, Sat noon–11pm 🚋 Tram 72

THE DECK ($$)

thedeckrestaurant.com.au

This European-style brasserie overlooking the Yarra gives commanding views of the city skyline and serves light meals with great coffee. It does a good breakfast and has an a la carte menu too.

➕ E7 ✉ Upper level, Southgate, Southbank ☎ 9699 9544 🕐 Mon–Thu 7.30am–10pm, Fri 7.30am–11pm, Sat noon–11pm, Sun noon–10pm 🚋 City Circle Tram

FRANCE SOIR ($$$)

france-soir.com.au

A Melbourne landmark for more than 20 years, France Soir is consistently popular for its exquisite renderings of classic French dishes and extensive and varied wine list. Reservations are a must.

➕ J12 ✉ 11 Toorak Road, South Yarra ☎ 9866 8569 🕐 Daily 12–12 🚋 Tram 58

GOOD EGG ($)

goodeggmelbourne.com.au

Come here for… ethical eggs! Done every which way, from miso soft boiled

LONG CHIM ($$)

longchimmlb.com

Chef David Thompson's Bangkok-style Thai street food can pack a chili punch. Riverside terrace dining with your choice of Thai dishes, including green papaya salad, pad Thai and grilled barramundi curry.

➕ D8 ✉ Crown Complex, 8 Whiteman Street ☎ 9292 5777 🕐 Wed, Thu, Sun noon–2.30 & 5.30–10pm, Fri & Sat noon–late 🚋 Tram 12, 96, 109

SAKÉ RESTAURANT HAMER HALL ($$)

sakerestaurant.com.au

Sit around the chef's kitchen or out on the terrace overlooking the Yarra to enjoy contemporary Japanese cuisine in the Hamer Hall, part of the Arts Centre. There's also a bento box-styled lunch menu to try.

➕ F7 ✉ Hamer Hall, 100 St. Kilda Road ☎ 8687 0775 🕐 Mon–Thu noon–3pm, 5–10pm, Fri & Sat noon–3pm, 5–11pm, Sun noon–10pm 🚋 Tram 3, 5, 6, 8

DINNER ON THE YARRA
What better way to experience Melbourne at night than a dinner cruise on the Yarra River? Hop aboard the *Spirit of Melbourne* cruising restaurant for a four-course meal with fabulous views, featuring the city skyline and docklands. Contact Melbourne River Cruises (☎ 8610 2600, melbcruises. com.au).

East Melbourne

Fringed by the lovely Fitzroy and Treasury Gardens, attractions east of the CBD include the famous Melbourne Cricket Ground and Richmond, one of Melbourne's oldest suburbs.

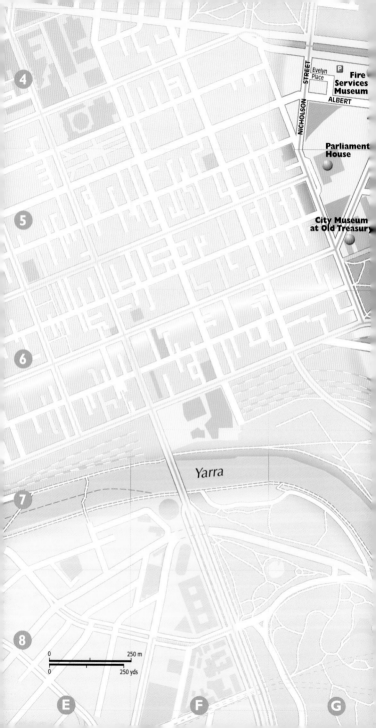

4

STREET

Evelyn
Place

P

**Fire
Services
Museum**

NICHOLSON

ALBERT

**Parliament
House**

5

**City Museum
at Old Treasury**

6

Yarra

7

8

0   250 m

0   250 yds

E   **F**   **G**

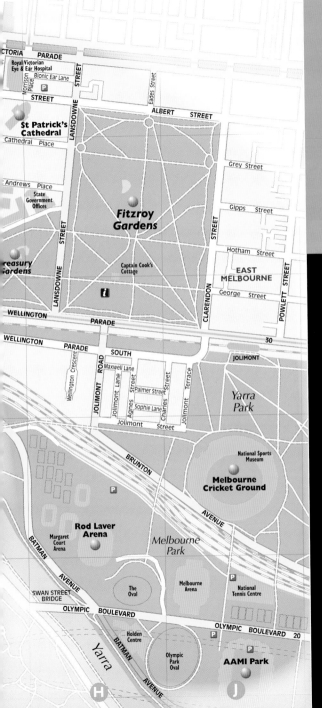

CTORIA PARADE

Royal Victorian
Eye & Ear Hospital Bionic Ear Lane

Morrison Place

STREET

St Patrick's
Cathedral

Cathedral Place

Andrews Place

State
Government
Offices

reasury
ardens

LANSDOWNE STREET

LANSDOWNE STREET

Eades Street

ALBERT STREET

Grey Street

Gipps Street

Fitzroy
Gardens

Captain Cook's
Cottage

Hotham Street

EAST
MELBOURNE

George Street

CLARENDON STREET

POWLETT STREET

WELLINGTON PARADE

WELLINGTON PARADE

PARADE SOUTH

JOLIMONT

30

Wellington Crescent

JOLIMONT ROAD

Maxwell Lane

Jolimont Lane

Agnes Street

Palmer Street

Sophie Lanes

Charles Street

Jolimont Terrace

Yarra
Park

Jolimont Street

BRUNTON

National Sports
Museum

Melbourne
Cricket Ground

AVENUE

Rod Laver
Arena

Margaret
Court
Arena

Melbourne
Park

BATMAN AVENUE

The
Oval

Melbourne
Arena

National
Tennis Centre

P

SWAN STREET
BRIDGE

OLYMPIC BOULEVARD

OLYMPIC BOULEVARD 20

Yarra

Holden
Centre

Olympic
Park
Oval

BATMAN AVENUE

AAMI Park

H

J

Fitzroy and Treasury Gardens

TOP **25**

The Tudor Village; Captain Cook's pretty English-style cottage

THE BASICS

fitzroygardens.com

✚ H5/G5

✉ Off Wellington Parade

☎ Cook's Cottage: 9658 9658

🕐 Cook's Cottage: daily 9–5. Tours Mon–Fri 10–2

🍴 Café

🚇 Jolimont

🚊 Tram 48, 75

♿ Cook's Cottage: inexpensive

HIGHLIGHTS

● Avenues of trees
● Conservatory
● Fairy Tree
● Model Tudor village
● Cook's Cottage
● John F. Kennedy Memorial

DID YOU KNOW?

The Wurundjeri people removed a piece of bark from the Scarred Tree, possibly to make a canoe, shelter or carrier. Similar scar trees can be found all over Australia.

The magnificent, tree-lined avenues of Fitzroy Gardens, designed in the 1850s, were accidentally laid out in the shape of a Union Jack flag. Across Lansdowne Road are the tranquil Treasury Gardens.

Fitzroy Gardens Fitzroy Gardens, with partly hidden glades, waterfalls and shady avenues of elms forming canopies across the pathways, is the location of Cook's Cottage. Also within the gardens is the Fairy Tree, whose trunk is carved with fantasy figures and Australian animals, a conservatory and the miniature Tudor Village, which was presented to Melbourne by the people of Lambeth, London, in appreciation of food packages sent to Britain after World War II. Keep an eye out for the Scarred Tree, an example of sustainable bushcraft by the Wurundjeri people, the traditional custodians of Melbourne.

Cook's Cottage This small English cottage, dating from 1755, was the home of the parents of navigator Captain James Cook. It was dismantled and shipped from Yorkshire to Melbourne in 1934 to be erected, stone by stone, on this site. It contains an interpretive area that explores the life of James Cook.

Treasury Gardens At lunchtime, city workers frequent this pleasant park planted with poplars, elms, oaks and cedars. There is a memorial to US President John F. Kennedy at the edge of the gardens' pretty ornamental lake, and a bronze statue of Scottish bard Robert Burns.

Some of the best moments in sporting history have happened at the "G"

Melbourne Cricket Ground

THE BASICS

mcg.org.au

➕ J7

✉ Brunton Avenue

☎ 9657 8888

🕐 National Sports Museum: daily 10–5. Tours: daily 10–3, hourly during events

🚆 Jolimont, Richmond

🚋 Tram 48, 70, 75

♿ Good

🚻 Moderate

Melbourne's shrine to sport, the "G" plays home to cricket and Aussie rules football, and was the focal point for the 1956 Olympics. Melburnians live for sport and this 100,000-seat stadium is where hearts have soared and been shattered in equal measure.

The hallowed ground Each week of the season, AFL football followers deck themselves out in their team colors and flock to the MCG. If you are in Melbourne, attend a football or cricket match and soak up the atmosphere—few stadiums in the world generate the excitement of the MCG. A guided tour is always a must: you can sit in the room where cricketers watch the game, visit the Long Room hung with portraits of cricketing greats, and inspect the memorabilia-packed Melbourne Cricket Club Museum. For many, a tour highlight is to stand on the famous playing field.

National Sports Museum Trace the history of the Olympic games via photographic displays of each of the modern Olympics, with priceless memorabilia and gold medals. Perhaps the best way to learn about cricket and Australian Rules Football (AFL) is to visit the Australian Gallery of Sport, in the same complex, which includes the Australian Cricket Hall of Fame and Australian Football Hall of Fame. There's also a thoroughbred racing gallery, and an interactive gallery where you can play virtual tennis and test your goal-kicking skills.

HIGHLIGHTS

- Standing on the oval
- Members' Pavilion
- Interactive games
- National Sports Museum
- Australian Gallery of Sport

DID YOU KNOW?

Of the 18 AFL teams, half are based in Melbourne, including Carlton, Collingwood, Essendon, Hawthorn, Melbourne, North Melbourne, Richmond and the mighty Western Bulldogs.

TIP

- If you're going to a cricket game, don't start a Mexican wave—it's prohibited!

EAST MELBOURNE TOP 25

More to See

AAMI PARK

aamipark.com.au

That spectacular bubbled dome on the side of the Yarra River is home to soccer clubs Melbourne Victory and Melbourne City, as well as rugby league Melbourne Storm and Super Rugby team Melbourne Rebels. Concerts take place here too. It's a magical sight at night when over 1,500 LED lights dance over its domes.

➕ J8 ✉ Olympic Boulevard, Melbourne Park ☎ 9286 1600 ⏰ Events only 🚊 Tram 48, 70, 75 ♿ Good 💷 Moderate

CITY MUSEUM AT OLD TREASURY

oldtreasurybuilding.org.au

This superb example of neoclassical architecture, one of the city's finest buildings, was built between 1858 and 1862 as the repository for the young colony's gold reserves. Now a museum, it showcases the wealth of the gold-rush era.

➕ G5 ✉ 20 Spring Street ☎ 9651 2233 ⏰ Sun–Fri 10–4 🚊 City Circle Tram 💷 Free

FIRE SERVICES MUSEUM

fsmv.net.au

On the first floor of a 19th-century fire station, this museum houses a collection of firefighting memorabilia such as uniforms and photographs, and includes Australia's largest collection of restored fire trucks. It's the biggest array of fire equipment in the southern hemisphere, spanning several hundred years.

➕ G4 ✉ 39 Gisborne Street ☎ 9662 2907 ⏰ Thu–Fri 9–3, Sun 10–4 🚊 City Circle Tram, 11, 12, 109 ♿ Few 💷 Inexpensive

PARLIAMENT HOUSE

parliament.vic.gov.au

Built during the gold rush in 1856, and amended with a wide flight of bluestone steps and towering Doric columns in 1892, this grand building was the first home of the Australian Parliament, until it moved to Canberra in 1927. You can attend a session when the State Parliament is sitting, and there are tours on weekdays.

AAMI Park

📍 G5 ✉ Spring Street ☎ 9651 8568
🕐 Mon–Fri 8.30–5.30 🚋 City Circle Tram
🎫 Free

RICHMOND

In Richmond, one of the city's oldest suburbs and a short tram ride from the CBD, you can find fashion outlets, with designer seconds, and some great bars and restaurants. Vietnamese culture thrives on Victoria Street, Melbourne's Little Saigon. Pop into the Richmond Football Club Museum at its Punt Road Oval ground in Yarra Park for all things "Tiger."

📍 Off map at J8 ✉ Bridge Road, Swan Street and Victoria Street 🍴 Many cafés and restaurants 🚋 Tram 48, 75, 109

ROD LAVER ARENA

rodlaverarena.com.au

One of Australia's largest sporting and entertainment venues is named after legendary Australian tennis player Rod Laver. Seating around 15,000, the arena attracts about a million visitors to events each year, including the annual prestigious Australian Open tennis event. It tops the list as a concert venue and has hosted big names like AC/DC, David Bowie, BB King, Oprah, Cher, Barry White, Lady Gaga, Janet Jackson, Pink… the list goes on.

📍 H7 ✉ Olympic Boulevard, Melbourne Park ☎ 9286 1600 🕐 Events only
🚉 Richmond 🚋 Tram 48, 70, 75
💰 Expensive

ST. PATRICK'S CATHEDRAL

cam.org.au/cathedral

You can see the spires of this 1897 bluestone Catholic cathedral from points all over the city. The interior has soaring, slender pillars, stained-glass windows and mosaic floor tiles. Exquisite glass mosaics are set into the marble and alabaster altars.

📍 G4 ✉ Cathedral Place ☎ 9662 2233
🕐 Mass Mon–Fri 7am & 1pm, Sat 8am & 6pm, Sun 8am, 9.30am, 11am & 6.30pm. Shop Mon–Fri 9.30–4.30, Sun 8.30–1 🚋 City Circle Tram, 11, 12, 109 🎫 Free

Detail from the community project mural in Stephenson Street, Richmond

Domestic Architecture Walk

Melbourne's architectural heritage includes examples of elaborate ironwork, bluestone facades and decorative brickwork.

DISTANCE: 5km (3 miles) **ALLOW:** 2 hours

START .... **END**

FEDERATION SQUARE
⊞ F7 🚋 City Circle Tram

SPRING STREET
⊞ G5 🚋 City Circle Tram

❶ Begin at Federation Square (▷ 42–43), then hop on a City Circle Tram or walk to the corner of Spring Street and Treasury Gardens. Walk into the gardens.

❽ Walk to Spring Street and catch the City Circle Tram to your next destination.

❷ Cross Lansdowne Street and pass the elegant 1930 conservatory on your way to Cook's Cottage. Continue toward Clarendon Street and cross into George Street.

❼ At the end of Hotham is the impressive Bishopscourt, built in 1853 as the home for Anglican archbishops. Take a break on the lawn under the elms in Fitzroy Gardens.

❸ Look for Hepburn Terrace at 199–209 George Street, a fine example of Victorian-era housing for the wealthy. Nearby, look for Nos. 193 and 188.

❻ Back on Powlett Street, Nos. 158–164, called Cyprus Terrace, were designed to appear as four houses, but are really two homes.

❹ These two well-restored 19th-century mansions are set opposite each other. Nearby, No. 182 dates from 1856. Cross Powlett Street to 109 George Street.

❺ Here you will see a small 1930s-era block of flats. Walk to Simpson Street, turn left, then left again into Hotham, with Queen Bess Row, built in 1886, and the adjacent Sydenham House, once a girls' school.

Shopping

BONDS OUTLET
bondsoutlet.com.au
This factory outlet sells Bonds clothing, alongside top fashion brands.
🔲 Off map ✉ 221 Bridge Road and Swan Street, Richmond ☎ 9427 8772 🕐 Daily 10–6 🚋 Tram 48, 75

MCG SHOP
mcgshop.com.au
Pick up Melbourne sporting memorabilia at the MCG shop.
🔲 J7 ✉ MCG, Brunton Avenue ☎ 9657 8860 🕐 Daily 10–5 🚋 Tram 48, 70, 75

RICHMOND HILL CAFÉ AND LARDER
rhcl.com.au
Fine condiments and fresh produce are for sale here, as well as a huge selection of cheeses in the Cheese Room.
🔲 Off map ✉ 48 Bridge Road, Richmond ☎ 9421 2808 🕐 Cheese Room: Mon–Thu 9–5, Fri & Sat 9–6, Sun 9–4 🚋 Tram 48, 75

Entertainment and Nightlife

ATLAS VINIFERA
atlasvinifera.com.au
Head to this cozy wine bar and bottle shop to enjoy the world's wine and snack on cheese and olives. Choose your own or let the owners guide you.
🔲 Off map ✉ 247 Church Street, Richmond ☎ 9428 6198 🕐 Sun–Wed 11am–9pm, Thu 11–10, Fri & Sat 11–11 🚉 Richmond 🚋 Tram 48, 75, 78

CORNER HOTEL
cornerhotel.com
A Melbourne live music institution, the Corner Hotel brings the best of all styles of local and international bands to Melbourne. It's got an adjoining rock 'n' roll pub and a huge roof-top bar.
🔲 Off map ✉ 57 Swan Street, Richmond ☎ 9427 7300 🕐 Tue–Sun noon–late 🚉 Richmond 🚋 Tram 70

SPREAD EAGLE HOTEL
spreadeagle.com.au
This bustling corner pub has a large beer, wine and spirit list, and a bistro serving traditional pub fare. There's live music on the weekend.
🔲 Off map ✉ 372 Bridge Road, Richmond ☎ 9428 6895 🕐 Sun–Thu noon–11pm, Fri & Sat noon–1am 🚋 Tram 48, 75

THE SWAN HOTEL
theswan.com.au
A traditional pub and the perfect venue to enjoy local live music and the footie finals. Serves great pub meals and has a spacious beer garden.
🔲 Off map ✉ 425 Church Street, Richmond ☎ 9428 2112 🕐 Daily noon–late 🚋 Tram 70, 78

POT AND A PARMA

Melburnians love a "pot and a parma," which translates as a glass of beer and a chicken parmigiana. The chicken is crumbed, fried and topped with a slice of ham, pasatta and cheese, then baked. It's a serious business—there's an annual award for the best. For vegetarians there's an equally delicious eggplant parma.

Where to Eat

BABY PIZZA ($$)

babypizza.com.au

A busy pizzeria with outdoor dining too, Baby has all foods Italian covered. Try small bites like parmesan polenta chips, or take on the pastas or gnocchi—just leave some room for *dolci*.

➕ Off map   ✉ 631 Church Street, Richmond   ☎ 9421 4599   ⏰ Daily 8am–late   🚊 Tram 78

BAHARI ($$)

bahari-richmond.com.au

A homey vibe welcomes you to Greek Bahari, where the menu encourages you to share with friends—fill up on dips, *saganaki*, slow-roasted lamb, Greek salad and baklava.

➕ Off map   ✉ 179 Swan Street, Richmond   ☎ 9427 7898   ⏰ Tue–Thu 5–10pm, Fri 5–11pm, Sat noon–11pm, Sun noon–10pm   🚉 East Richmond   🚊 Tram 70, 78

HARD PRESSED COFFEE ($)

hardpressedcoffee.com.au

Specialty coffee—espresso, filter, French press and cold brew—is the highlight of this café. All-day brunch and generous sandwiches are also available.

➕ Off map at J6   ✉ 76 Wellington Parade   ☎ 9417 4441   ⏰ Mon–Fri 7–4, Sat & Sun 8–3   🚊 Tram 48, 75

MEATBALL & WINE BAR ($)

meatballandwinebar.com.au

This place is all about meatballs, including veg and fish options. Choose your sauce and something for them to sit on—mash, beans or pasta—and you're now a baller.

➕ Off map   ✉ 105 Swan Street, Richmond   ☎ 9428 3339   ⏰ Mon & Tue 5pm–late, Wed–Sun noon–late   🚉 Richmond   🚊 Tram 70

NOIR ($$$)

noirrestaurant.com.au

Noir offers a minimalist space with black-painted walls and romantic lighting. Modern French cuisine is served accompanied by wines by the glass.

➕ Off map   ✉ 175 Swan Street, Richmond   ☎ 9428 3585   ⏰ Tue–Sun 6–10pm, also Fri & Sun noon–3pm   🚊 Tram 48, 75

ONDA ($)

ondamelbourne.com

Take a seat on a blue velvety wave-shaped couch and prepare to eat from a modern Latin American menu with a few twists.

➕ Off map   ✉ 280 Bridge Road, Richmond   ☎ 9429 8589   ⏰ Wed–Sun noon–10.30pm   🚊 Tram 48, 75, 78

TRAN TRAN ($)

trantran.com.au

For almost 30 years Tran Tran has been a stayer on the Vietnamese strip of Victoria Street. The space shows off its original 1890s chapel ceiling, and the food is as authentic as it gets.

➕ Off map   ✉ 74 Victoria Street, Richmond   ☎ 9429 6147   ⏰ Daily 11.30am–9.30pm   🚉 North Richmond   🚊 Tram 12, 109

VICTORIAN WINES
It's worth seeking out Victorian wines to go with your food, particularly those from the Yarra Valley and Macedon Ranges. Wines from the Yarra Valley include Chardonnay and Pinot Noir; Macedon Ranges include Merlot and Cabernet Sauvignon.

Carlton and Fitzroy

These lively inner-city suburbs are easily reached by tram from the CBD. Carlton, with its excellent museum, has eateries, bookshops and galleries, while Fitzroy has an alternative atmosphere.

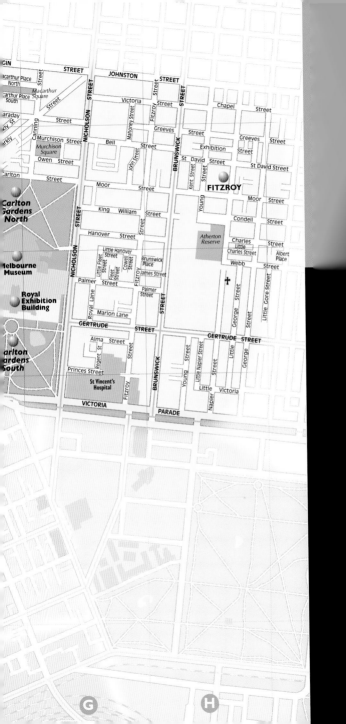

Carlton

Carlton is popular for eating out—Lygon Street (left) and interior of D.O.C. Espresso (right)

THE BASICS

➕ E2

✉ Lygon Street, Rathdowne Street

🍴 Many cafés and restaurants

🚊 Tram 1, 6

HIGHLIGHTS

- Italian culture
- Restaurants
- Nightlife
- Specialty shopping
- Melbourne Museum
- Carlton Gardens
- Royal Exhibition Building

DID YOU KNOW?

Aussie Rules' Carlton Football Club is one of the world's oldest, founded in 1864 and one of the foundation clubs of the Victorian Football League, formed in 1897. Nicknamed the Navy Blues, the club have won 16 VFL/AFL premierships, the most of any club bar rivals Essendon.

Carlton has long been dubbed the city's Little Italy. Centered around bustling Lygon Street, with its alfresco dining scene, the area is also home to fabulous gardens, and an art-house cinema and theater.

Tasty Italian Carlton's Italian origins date from the early 1900s, when Italian migrants settled here, and were boosted with post-World War II migration. It is the perfect near-city destination for a gastronomic expedition, since there are any number of excellent eating places to tempt you, many based in old double-storied Victorian terraced houses.

Art-house entertainment Catch a performance at La Mama Theatre (▷ 89), one of Melbourne's original experimental theaters—productions are often new works showcasing up-and-coming writers and actors. Cinema Nova (▷ 89) is Carlton's home of art-house film.

Shopping Besides delicious Italian fare, on a leisurely stroll you'll find boutiques, specialty men's and women's clothing stores, and jewelry and gift shops. Lygon Street has one of the best bookshops in Melbourne, Readings (▷ 88).

Piazzas At the northern end of Argyle Street is Piazza Italia, with gardens, stone paving and a huge solar clock. Here you can sit in the sun, close your eyes, and dream of being in Italy. Come here for the Italian Festival held each year in October (carltonitalianfesta.org.au).

Bohemian lifestyles and festival parades are central to the suburb of Fitzroy

Fitzroy

In the heart of Fitzroy, Brunswick Street rolls to an alternative beat with its live music, art, grunge bars and upmarket wine bars, and myriad multicultural restaurants.

Live music For every block on Brunswick, Johnston and Gertrude streets there's a bar or venue playing live music. Lots of performances are free, but shout the band a pint or two as local musicians rarely get paid their due. For gigs check out *Beat* magazine (beat.com.au/gig-guide).

Art scene Head to Gertrude Street, where Melbourne's emerging artists show their work. You'll also find some retro fashion and cutting-edge clothing shops here. It's a great place to buy books, art, antiques and the latest retro fashions.

Multicultural The area is occupied by some of Melbourne's vibrant subcultures, including students and artists, along with inner-city urbanites attracted by the suburb's eclectic nature. Part of the fun of hanging out here is to sit with a coffee and people-watch. Melbourne's Spanish community is based in Johnson Street, where you'll find tapas bars; you'll also find food of every variety—Turkish, Greek, Italian, Thai, Malaysian, Vietnamese, Tibetan, African, and the list continues to grow. There are plenty of restaurants featuring Modern Australian cuisine, too.

THE BASICS

- H2
- Brunswick Street
- Cafés and restaurants
- Tram 11
- Fair

HIGHLIGHTS

- People-watching
- Bric-a-brac shops
- Designer clothes shops
- Nightlife
- Art galleries

DID YOU KNOW?

Fitzroy is the heart of Aboriginal Melbourne's social and political scene. Go to aboriginalhistory ofyarra.com.au and download the Fitzroy Aboriginal Heritage Walking Trail map that takes you around 16 places of great significance and explains the Indigenous Australian history of the area.

Melbourne Museum

● Bunjilaka Aboriginal Cultural Centre
● Children's Discovery Centre
● IMAX cinema
● Forest Gallery
● Science Gallery
● Te Pasifika Gallery

This ultra-modern museum, which claims to be the largest in the southern hemisphere, features the art, culture and natural history of Melbourne and the surrounding area, using interaction, performance and the latest technology.

Museum exhibitions Major touring exhibitions supplement the collections of this museum in Carlton Gardens, opposite the grand 19th-century Royal Exhibition Building. The Melbourne Gallery focuses primarily on the city's history. The Bunjilaka Aboriginal Cultural Centre tells the stories of Victorian Aboriginal people, and explores the land and issues relating to Aboriginal laws, traditional knowledge and property. Te Pasifika Gallery houses art from many Pacific countries.

Clockwise from far left: the Dinosaur Walk; painted panels by Aboriginal artist Gaymala Yunipingu in the Lower Gallery; an exhibition at Bunjilaka Aboriginal Cultural Centre; the exterior of Melbourne Museum

Our world In the Forest Gallery you walk among living trees, plants, animals, birds and insects; interpretive zones explain the effects of fire, water, earth movement, climate and humans on the forests around Melbourne. Exhibitions in the Science and Life Gallery, including several dinosaur and other prehistoric skeletons, show how much science shapes our world. Technology exhibitions explore the rapid evolution of digital technology and its dramatic effects on our daily lives. Check out the intricate workings of human beings in the popular Mind and Body Gallery.

Family fun Nearby at the Children's Museum, kids and their families are encouraged to engage with interactive exhibitions. The IMAX cinema, shops and cafés are in the complex.

THE BASICS

museumvictoria.com.au/ melbournemuseum

🚩 F3

✉ 11 Nicholson Street, Carlton Gardens, Carlton

☎ 13 11 02

🕐 Daily 10–5

🍴 Cafés and restaurant

🚃 City Circle Tram, 86, 96

♿ Excellent

💵 Inexpensive

❓ Daily guided tours

IMAX theater

imaxmelbourne.com.au

✉ Melbourne Museum Precinct

☎ 9663 5454

More to See

CARLTON GARDENS

melbourne.vic.gov.au/parks

These gardens are well laid out with public art, a huge fountain and avenues of mature trees. In the center is the Royal Exhibition Building (▷ right). Next to Carlton Gardens, in Nicholson Street, is a restored row of terraced houses, known as Royal Terrace. The innovative Melbourne Museum is to the north.

⊞ F2/F3 ⊠ Between Rathdowne and Nicholson streets 🚋 Tram 86, 96 🎟 Free

GRAINGER MUSEUM

grainger.unimelb.edu.au

Musician and composer Percy Grainger, famous for his arrangement of folk tune "Country Gardens," began this autobiographical and music museum in the 1930s. Part of the University of Melbourne's Cultural Collections, you could easily lose a few hours here. He invented many a musical instrument; you can see them alongside guitars, gramophones and pianos.

⊞ D1 ⊠ Gate 13, Royal Parade, Parkville
☎ 8344 5270 🕐 Sun–Fri noon–4pm
🍴 Several cafés 🚋 Tram 19 ♿ Excellent
🎟 Free ❓ Guided tours last 45 minutes and cost $5. Reserve online.

ROYAL EXHIBITION BUILDING

museumvictoria.com.au/reb

A UNESCO World Heritage building, this magnificent structure was built for the International Exhibition of 1880 and remains the world's oldest surviving structure of its type.

⊞ F3 ⊠ Nicholson Street, Carlton
☎ 13 11 02 🕐 Tours daily 🚋 Trams 86, 96
🎟 Inexpensive

UNIVERSITY OF MELBOURNE

unimelb.edu.au

Wander around these attractive grounds and admire the buildings, including Ormond College (1880), with its Gothic tower, and Newman College, designed in 1918 by the architect Walter Burley Griffin.

⊞ D1 ⊠ Grattan Street, Parkville ☎ 13 63 52 🕐 Daily 🍴 Several cafés 🚋 Tram 1, 3, 5, 6, 16, 19, 64, 67, 72 🎟 Free

Carlton Gardens are home to the modern Melbourne Museum

Royal Exhibition Building, Carlton Gardens

Carlton Gardens to Swanston Street

An interesting walk that includes the grand old Royal Exhibition Building, the Melbourne Museum and bustling Lygon Street.

DISTANCE: 3km (2 miles) **ALLOW:** 3 hours

START

CARLTON GARDENS
F3 Tram 86, 96

END

SWANSTON STREET
E2 Trams 1, 3, 6, 16, 64, 67, 72

1 Begin at Carlton Gardens South on the corner of Victoria and Rathdowne streets, walk diagonally across toward the Royal Exhibition Building (▷ 86), to the Hochgurtel Fountain, with its three colossal half-man, half-fish figures.

8 From here you can walk through Argyle Square and out onto Swanston Street to catch a tram back into the CBD.

2 Walk to the east around the building past the French fountain, with its three figures supporting dolphins, to take in the scale of this impressive building.

7 Make your way southward, along Lygon Street, to the intersection of Pelham and Lygon streets, where you'll find the Piazza Italia and the adjacent pretty Argyle Square.

3 Just opposite is the dramatic Melbourne Museum (▷ 84). You can't miss the huge indoor forest as you enter the building.

6 At 380 Lygon Street, there is a good collection of specialty shops in the Lygon Court Shopping Piazza, which also houses one of Melbourne's finest art-house cinemas, Cinema Nova (▷ 89).

4 Now walk westward past the IMAX theater and the colorful cube building into the northern section of Carlton Gardens (▷ 86).

5 Walk down Rathdowne Street, turn left into Grattan Street, then walk the two blocks to Lygon Street.

CARLTON AND FITZROY WALK

Shopping

KOKO BLACK

kokoblack.com

A chocolate indulgence, where some 100 delicious handmade chocolates await, the only problem is choosing which ones to buy. Best to go for a chocolate gift box and pack it full of Amarena cherry or Belgian truffle or caramel mousse or…

⊞ E2 ✉ 167 Lygon Street, Carlton ☎ 9349 2882 🕙 Daily 10–10 🚋 Tram 1, 3, 5, 6, 16, 64, 67, 72

MAKE DESIGNED OBJECTS

makedesignedobjects.com

You can't help but buy something at this design store as kitchenware, homeware, jewelry or bedding will end up with you at the check out. Find quality local and internationally designed objects from littala, Rosendahl, Fink & Co, Menu, Eva Solo and much more.

⊞ F1 ✉ 194 Elgin Street, Carlton ☎ 9347 4225 🕙 Mon–Thu 10–5.30, Fri 10–7, Sat 10–5.30 🚋 Tram 1, 6

MUSIC SWOP SHOP

musicswopshop.com.au

Lots of secondhand and rare musical instruments are for sale here; also custom instrument design and the best place to head to for repairs.

⊞ F1 ✉ 147 Elgin Street, Carlton ☎ 9348 1194 🕙 Mon–Fri 11–6, Sat & Sun 11–3 🚋 Tram 1, 6

THE ORIGINAL LOLLY STORE

theoriginallollystore.com.au

Lollies from around the world, including American, English and Dutch sweets, European chocolates, plus good old Australian favorites. Jelly babies, fudge, licorice, chocolates and also sodas are all up for grabs.

⊞ E2 ✉ 239 Lygon Street, Carlton ☎ 1300 456 559 🕙 Mon–Thu 11–10, Fri 11–11, Sat 11am–11.30pm, Sun 12.15pm–10pm 🚋 Tram 1, 6

POLYESTER

polyesterrecords.com

This independent record store stocks a huge range of vinyl, CDs, DVDs and books. It has in-store live music and album launches, too.

⊞ Off map ✉ 387 Brunswick Street, Fitzroy ☎ 9419 5137 🕙 Mon–Thu, Sat 11–7, Fri 11–8, Sun 11–5 🚋 Tram 11

READINGS

readings.com.au

One of Melbourne's top bookshops, Readings sells an excellent range of the latest titles and CDs. Frequently holds book launches and talks.

⊞ E2 ✉ 309 Lygon Street, Carlton ☎ 9347 6633 🚋 Tram 1, 6

ROSE STREET ARTISTS' MARKET

rosestmarket.com.au

Home to some of Melbourne's best artists and designers, find high-quality, locally designed jewelry, clothes, accessories, art, vintage pieces, collectibles, homewares and soft furnishings here.

⊞ Off map ✉ 60 Rose Street, Fitzroy ☎ 9419 5529 🕙 Sat–Sun 11–5 🚋 Tram 11

ZETTA FLORENCE

zettaflorence.com.au

Vintage prints and original designs adorn the covers of journals, notebooks and writing sets, as well as wrapping and decorative papers. The place to come for a one-of-a-kind greeting card.

⊞ H2 ✉ 197B Brunswick Street, Fitzroy ☎ 9039 5583 🕙 Mon–Fri 10–6, Sat 10–5, Sun 11–5 🚋 Tram 11

Entertainment and Nightlife

CINEMA NOVA

cinemanova.com.au

This art-house cinema complex offers top new-release art-house and commercial films, special film festivals and events. It's a fully licensed venue.

F1 ✉ 380 Lygon Street, Carlton ☎ 9347 5531 🚊 Tram 1, 6

EVELYN HOTEL

evelynhotel.com.au

This grungy hotel has a beer garden and band room that hosts live band music most nights, plus a front bar with a big screen and pool table.

H1 ✉ 351 Brunswick Street, Fitzroy ☎ 9419 5500 🕑 Daily 12.30pm–1.30am 🚊 Tram 11

THE EVERLEIGH

theeverleigh.com

Head upstairs to a bygone-era bar and settle into a booth for exquisite cocktails. Go with the Bartender's Choice.

H3 ✉ Upstairs, 150–156 Gertrude Street, Fitzroy ☎ 9416 2229 🕑 Daily 5pm–1am 🚊 Tram 86

IMAX

imaxmelbourne.com.au

The screen is the world's largest at 32 meters (105ft) wide and 23 meters (75ft) high, the projectors and sound systems are state-of-the-art, and the movies are specially made to suit.

F3 ✉ Melbourne Museum, Carlton ☎ 9663 5454 🚊 City Circle Tram, 1, 86, 96

LA MAMA THEATRE

lamama.com.au

A not-for-profit theater and one of the city's principal venues for showcasing contemporary Australian theater. It's an innovative space that champions diversity and supporting the community.

F1 ✉ 205 Faraday Street, Carlton ☎ 9347 6948 🚊 Tram 1, 6

JIMMY WATSON'S WINE BAR

jimmywatsons.com

A wine bar, bistro and restaurant, this Melbourne institution has long been the place to socialize and sample wines of great quality. Sit at the traditional bar, or head up to the rooftop.

F1 ✉ 333 Lygon Street, Carlton ☎ 9347 3985 🕑 Daily 11am–late 🚊 Tram 1, 6

MILK THE COW

milkthecow.com.au

A cheese bar that pairs champagne wine, whiskey, beer and other spirits is a match made in heaven. Order what you fancy and staff will tell you the story behind each cheese. Just be sure to get there early.

F1 ✉ 323 Lygon Street, Carlton ☎ 9348 4771 🕑 Daily noon–late 🚊 Tram 1, 6

NAKED FOR SATAN

nakedforsatan.com.au

The downstairs bar serves little bites, vodka, beer and wine. On the roof, via an old lift shaft, is Naked in the Sky, with a bar, lounge, restaurant and terrace with killer views of Fitzroy and the city.

H1 ✉ 285 Brunswick Street, Fitzroy ☎ 9416 2238 🕑 Fri–Sat noon–1am, Sun–Thu noon–late 🚊 Tram 11

THE CINEMA SCENE

The main complexes are at Melbourne Central, the Jam Factory and Crown Entertainment Complex. More alternative cinemas include the Astor in St. Kilda and Kino at Collins Place. For foreign and art-house films try the Cinema Nova in Carlton on Lygon Street. Schedules are online and in *The Age* and *Herald Sun*.

Where to Eat

PRICES	
Prices are approximate, based on a 3-course meal for one person.	
$	A$25–A$45
$$	A$46–A$75
$$$	A$76–A$120

BLUE CHILLIES ($$)
bluechillies.com.au
This stylish Malaysian restaurant with hawker-style menu offerings serves all the old favorites, including *laksas* and *nasi goreng*.
➕ H2 ✉ 182 Brunswick Street, Fitzroy ☎ 9417 0071 🕐 Mon–Thu noon–3pm, 5–10pm, Fri & Sat noon–3pm, 5–11pm, Sun 5–11pm 🚊 Tram 11

D.O.C. ESPRESSO ($$)
docgroup.net
D.O.C. serves great coffee and classic Italian pasta and pizza. Head here early for a breakfast foccacia. There's another branch around the corner.
➕ F1 ✉ 326 Lygon Street, Carlton ☎ 9347 8482 🕐 Mon–Sat 7am–late, Sun 8am–late 🚊 Tram 1

EPOCHA ($$)
epocha.com.au
Have a traditional Sunday roast in a Victorian terrace overlooking Carlton Gardens. Add to that quality European tasting menus and you're all set for lunch and dinner.
➕ F3 ✉ 49 Rathdowne Street, Carlton ☎ 9036 4949 🕐 Mon–Wed 5.30pm–late, Thu–Sat noon–3pm & 5.30pm–late, Sun noon–3pm 🚊 Tram 86, 96

HEART ATTACK AND VINE ($)
heartattackandvine.com.au
Start the day with a European breakfast and specialty coffee or aim for a generous lunch at this espresso bar/café. It's open for dinner too.
➕ F1 ✉ 329 Lygon Street, Carlton ☎ 9005 8624 🕐 Mon–Fri 7am–11pm, Sat & Sun 8am–11pm 🚊 Tram 1, 6

HOOKED FITZROY ($)
hookedfishandchipper.com.au
Fresh fish and hand-cut chips, plus daily specials are on offer here. Sit in at communal tables or take out.
➕ Off map ✉ 384 Brunswick Street, Fitzroy ☎ 9417 7740 🕐 Thu–Sat noon–10, Sun–Wed noon–9.30 🚊 Tram 11

SMITH & DAUGHTERS ($$)
smithanddaughters.com
Small and big vegan plates make up a sublime menu filled with familiar sounding dishes—all plant-based. Top it off with an equally delicious dessert.
➕ H2 ✉ 175 Brunswick Street, Fitzroy ☎ 9939 3293 🕐 Tue–Fri 6pm–late, Sat 10am–late, Sun 10am–11pm 🚊 Tram 11

TIAMO ($)
tiamo.com.au
Classic Italian that's been the heart of Melbourne's Little Italy for over 30 years. Pizza, pasta and parmigiana are all on the menu, there's a sweet dessert list and every type of coffee imaginable.
➕ F1 ✉ 303 Lygon Street, Carlton ☎ 9347 5759 🕐 Mon–Fri 11–10, Sat 9.30am–10pm, Sun 9am–10pm 🚊 Tram 1, 6

VEGIE BAR ($)
vegiebar.com.au
For over 20 years this busy vegetarian restaurant has been cooking up sensational food that's great for the body and soul. Choose from stir-fries, curries, pizzas, burgers and wholefood bowls.
➕ Off map ✉ 380 Brunswick Street, Fitzroy ☎ 9417 6935 🕐 Daily 11am–late 🚊 Tram 11

Farther Afield

Take a trip to the attractions in the city's outer suburbs—head east to the seaside suburb of St. Kilda or west to Scienceworks in Spotswood. Melbourne is handy for day trips farther afield to the Great Ocean Road and Yarra Valley, too.

↑ Melbourne Tullamarine Airport

PASCOE VALE

ESSENDON NORTH

BELL STREET

COBURG

ESSENDON

Merri Creek

MOONEE PONDS

MARIBYRNONG ROAD

SYDNEY ROAD

CERES Community Environment Park

BRUNSWICK

BRUNSWICK ROAD

ROAD

Maribyrnong

PARKVILLE

Melbourne Zoo

Royal Park

FLEMINGTON

HIGHWAY)

Melbourne General Cemeter

Flemington Racecourse

(PRINCES

BALLARAT ROAD

FLEMINGTON ROAD

ROYAL PARADE

STREET

ALEXANDRA PARADE

CARLTON

NICHOLSON

COLLIN WOOD

GEELONG ROAD (PRINCES HIGHWAY)

DYNON ROAD

FOOTSCRAY

FOOTSCRAY ROAD

NORTH MELBOURNE

FITZROY

WILLIAMSTOWN ROAD

WHITEHALL STREET

CITYLINK

Yarra

MELBOURNE

Yarra Park

Melbourne Park

RAAF Museum Point Cook

WESTGATE

FREEWAY

CITYLINK

Kings Domain

KINGS WAY

Scienceworks

PORT MELBOURNE

SOUTH MELBOURNE

ST KILDA ROAD

Fawkner Park

QUEENS ROAD

PUNT ROAD

NEWPORT

ALBERT PARK

Albert Park

MELBOURNE ROAD

BEACONSFIELD

Albert Park Lake

MIDDLE PARK

PARADE

Jewish Museum of Australia

WILLIAMSTOWN

Port Phillip Bay

ST KILDA

Luna Park

ELWOOD

0   2 km

0   2 miles

Heide Museum of Modern Art

TOP
25

Modern buildings and abstract sculpture reflecting the style of art found here

THE BASICS

heide.com.au
🔳 See map ▷ 93
✉ 7 Templestowe Road, Bulleen
☎ 9850 1500
🕐 Tue–Sun 10–5
🍴 Café Heide
🚉 Heidelberg
🚌 From station, take bus 903 and alight near the museum
♿ Good
💲 Moderate
❓ Free guided tour at 2pm

HIGHLIGHTS

● Contemporary art
● Walks
● Sculpture garden
● Heide store

Celebrating the work of Australia's early modernists, this very special museum and its riverbank sculpture gardens were once the stomping ground of a new generation of artists, whose aim was nothing short of revolutionizing Australian art.

The gallery Set on the banks of the Yarra River, Heide first belonged to John and Sunday Reed, whose patronage, beginning in the 1930s, nurtured a new generation of outstanding artists. Starting with a run-down dairy farm, the Reeds built a fine contemporary home and created an inspiring environment in which artists could meet and work.

Modern art Today these buildings house a permanent collection of Australian modernists—paintings by Arthur Boyd, Charles Blackman, Joy Hester, Sidney Nolan, Albert Tucker, Peter Booth and Jenny Watson, and sculptures by Rick Amor and Stephen Killick. The free tour gives insights into the lives of the artists influenced by the Reeds.

The garden Stroll around the parklands and picnic in the grounds and along the riverbank. The rambling park comprises native and European trees and has a well-tended kitchen garden and sculpture gardens running right down to the Yarra River. Or try the café at the entrance to the museum. Temporary exhibitions and events offer perspectives on aspects of Australian art.

Giraffes, bathing elephants and lowland gorillas are just some of the creatures at the zoo

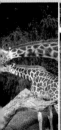

Gorillas and elephants get top billing here, but the otters, kangaroos, koalas and wombats are just as fascinating. The platypus is also represented, together with much of Australia's unique birdlife.

Background This popular zoo, the oldest in Australia, was established in 1862 in Royal Park. At first the zoo was used for domestic livestock; after 1870, more exotic animals were collected for display.

Australian fauna Platypuses caper in the nocturnal display and koalas sleep high up in the trees. Tasmanian devils feature and you can learn about the struggle to save them from extinction. There's a wombat burrow and out in the bushland, kangaroos, emus and wallabies hang out. The Aussie fur seal is also here.

Around the world The gorillas have their own rainforest and you can come face-to-face with the king of the jungle in Lion Gorge. See Sumatran tigers and orangutans, plus Asian elephants in the elephants village and garden.

Royal Park The Zoo is the focal point of this park where green open spaces, gardens of native plants and groves of smooth eucalyptus trees make you feel far from busy Melbourne. Look for the memorial cairn to Burke and Wills, commemorating the starting point for the fateful crossing of the Australian interior in 1860. There are sports facilities here too.

Rippon Lea House and Como House

TOP 25

The Romanesque Rippon Lea House (left) and elegant Como House (right)

THE BASICS

Rippon Lea House
ripponleaestate.com.au
➕ See map ▷ 93
✉ 192 Hotham Street, Elsternwick
☎ 9523 6095
🕐 Daily 10–5
🚋 Tram 67
♿ Inexpensive
❓ Guided tours daily

Como House
nationaltrust.org.au/places/como-house-and-garden
➕ See map ▷ 93
✉ Corner of Williams Road and Lechlade Avenue, South Yarra
☎ 9656 9889
🕐 Gardens Mon–Sat 9–5, Sun 10–5
🚋 Tram 8
♿ Inexpensive
❓ House tours Wed 2pm, Sat & Sun 11am, 12.30pm, 2pm

HIGHLIGHTS

- Unique architecture
- Park-like grounds
- Fountain terrace
- Stunning interiors

Managed by the National Trust, these outstanding examples of 19th-century suburban estates are just a few miles apart, south of the Yarra River. Their magnificent gardens are intact and the architecture is very well preserved.

Rippon Lea House The ornate, Romanesque Rippon Lea House, built in 1868 with distinctive polychome bricks and extended in 1897, has 36 opulent rooms where Victorian splendor mixes with the 1930s tastes of its last owner. The fine 5.7ha (14-acre) Victorian pleasure garden includes an orchard, desert garden, ornamental lake with islands and decorative bridges, a 19th-century conservatory and grand Victorian fernery. Bring a picnic lunch or have a coffee at the Gatehouse tearooms, then spend the afternoon touring the mansion and relaxing by the lake. Access to the house is by tour only, so reserve ahead.

Como House Two hectares (5 acres) of gardens surround this elegant home, built between 1847 and 1859, in an unusual mix of Australian Regency and Italianate styles. This gracious building perfectly exemplifies the wealthy landowner lifestyle in mid-19th-century Australia. The original kitchen outbuilding and laundry remain. Sloping lawns, flower gardens and pine and cypress glades make up the grounds; there's also a croquet lawn, a fountain terrace and a water garden by 19th-century landscape designer Ellis Stones.

A stunning aerial view of St. Kilda, with the magical Luna Park at its heart

St. Kilda and Luna Park

A wander along St. Kilda's Esplanade and Pier affords some stunning views of Port Phillip Bay. Melbourne's seaside playground is also home to some of the city's best restaurants and bars, as well as super-fun rides at Luna Park.

The beach Since Melbourne's early days people have flocked to this beachside suburb, 6.5km (4 miles) southeast of the city, to enjoy the cool sea breezes off Port Phillip Bay. Late in the 19th century, the wealthy built large houses in the area, away from the heat of the city. The beaches are fine for swimming, although there can be an undertow. Windsurfing is popular.

The streets Fitzroy and Acland streets are a mix of retail and dining establishments, lively bars and art galleries. Many of the grand old buildings have been restored and the charm of the place is immense. On Sundays an open-air arts and crafts market draws huge crowds.

St. Kilda Pier This popular pier, erected in 1857, is about 150m (164 yards) from the beach end of Fitzroy Street. From the end of the pier you can see the grand sweep of the bay around to Port Melbourne.

Luna Park Built in 1912, this St. Kilda institution is one of the oldest amusement parks in the world with its continually running Great Scenic Railway roller coaster. The popular carousel dates back to the park's earliest days.

THE BASICS

St. Kilda
stkildamelbourne.com.au
➕ See map ▷ 92
🕐 24 hours daily
🚋 Tram 3, 12, 16, 96
♿ Good
🎟 Free

Luna Park
lunapark.com.au
➕ See map ▷ 92
☎ 9525 5033
🕐 Fri 7am–11pm, Sat 11–11, Sun 11–8. Daily during school holidays
🍴 Food stalls
🚋 Trams 16, 96
🎟 Moderate–expensive

HIGHLIGHTS

● Swimming in summer
● Cafés on Fitzroy and Acland streets
● Patisseries
● Walking on the pier or along the beach
● St. Kilda Botanical Gardens
● Nightlife

Scienceworks

TOP 25

Hands-on and action packed—the exciting Scienceworks museum caters for all ages

THE BASICS

museumvictoria.com.au/
scienceworks
➕ See map ▷ 92
✉ 2 Booker Street,
Spotswood
☎ 13 11 02
🕐 Daily 10–4.30
🍴 Café
🚆 Spotswood
⛴ Ferry from Southbank
♿ Inexpensive
❓ Daily tours

HIGHLIGHTS

● Hands-on exhibits
● Planetarium shows
● Temporary exhibits
● Old steam pumps

This hands-on science and technology museum is an exciting showcase of science past, present and future. For a fast, digital trip around the universe, visit the adjacent Planetarium.

Exhibitions At "Sportsworks" you can stretch your mind and your muscles. Try the extreme snowboarding experience and the 3D soccer goalie game. Here you can discover your sporting talents and profile. "Think Ahead" displays hundreds of objects from the past, present and speculative future. High-tech meets hands-on to give a projection of future Earth and its lifestyles. "Beyond Perception: Seeing the Unseen" delves into the hidden forces and fields around us, and answers questions about gravity, aerodynamics, light and sound.

Planetarium A great range of shows at this digital planetarium re-creates the night sky and gives you a close-up look at the moon, the stars and our planets. The Planetarium has a 16m (52ft) domed ceiling, reclining seats, a stereo surround-sound system, and a high-resolution projection system that presents an unforgettable and awe-inspiring astronomical experience.

The Pumping Station One of Australia's most important industrial heritage sites, the Pumping Station has giant working steam-driven pumps, now driven by compressed air. These were a key component of the city's first centralized sewerage system.

More to See

ABBOTSFORD CONVENT

abbotsfordconvent.com.au

Historic Abbotsford Convent is another of Melbourne's arts precincts, this time over 11 historic buildings and gardens. Come here for exhibitions at the galleries, or pop in on a weekend to one of its many markets—book, vegan and farmers'. Learn about the fascinating history of the site, from Wurundjeri meeting point to convent to university to non-profit art space.

🔲 See map ▷ 93 ⬚ 1 St Heliers Street, Abbotsford ☎ 9415 3600 ⏰ Daily 7.30am–10pm 🍴 Cam's, Convent Bakery, Bar & Pizzeria, Kappaya Japanese Soul Food, Lentil as Anything 🚆 Victoria Park 🚋 Tram 109 ♿ Good 🎫 Free; donations welcome. Tour on Sunday at 2pm, inexpensive

CARLTON BREWHOUSE

carltonbrewhouse.com.au

Visit Carlton Brewhouse for a tour of an Australian brewery. It includes a look at the production, bottling and keg lines, before returning to the tasting room to sample different beers. There is a café for refreshments. Reservations are essential.

🔲 See map ▷ 93 ⬚ Corner of Nelson and Thompson streets, Abbotsford ☎ 9420 6800 ⏰ Tue & Wed 10–4, Thu & Fri 10am–late, Sat 10–4, Sun 11.30–6.30 🚋 Tram 109 🎫 Moderate ❓ Beer & Food, Beer 101, Tasting tours

CERES (COMMUNITY ENVIRONMENT PARK)

ceres.org.au

Set alongside the pretty Merri Creek, non-profit CERES is all about sustainability and community. Visit the 4-acre nursery, pop into the grocery shop and enjoy an organic breakfast or lunch at the environmentally friendly café. Every Saturday there's a flea market with music and lots of up-cycled and sustainable things to buy.

🔲 See map ▷ 93 ⬚ Corner of Roberts & Stewart streets, Brunswick East ☎ 9389 0100 ⏰ Daily 9–5 🍴 The Merri Table 🚋 Tram 96 ♿ Few 🎫 Free; donations welcome

COLLINGWOOD CHILDREN'S FARM

farm.org.au

Come here to cuddle guinea pigs, feed chickens, groom horses and even learn how to milk a cow. There's fun on this farm for the whole family—and it's only a short train ride from the CBD. Pick up a picnic basket from the Farm Café and enjoy it on the grounds. Second Saturday of the month there's a huge farmers' market.

🔲 See map ▷ 93 ⬚ 18 St Heliers Street, Abbotsford ☎ 9417 5806 ⏰ Daily 9.15–4.30 🍴 The Farm Café 🚆 Victoria Park ♿ Few 🎫 Inexpensive

Abbotsford Convent

JEWISH MUSEUM OF AUSTRALIA

jewishmuseum.com.au

Dedicated to the conservation, preservation and exhibition of Jewish heritage, this museum presents the Australian–Jewish experience. You'll find state-of-the-art interactive displays helping to explain the Jewish year, beliefs and rituals.

➕ See map ▷ 92   ✉ 26 Alma Road, St. Kilda   ☎ 8534 3600   ⏰ Tue–Thu 10–4, Fri 10–3, Sun 10–5   🚋 Tram 3, 67   💲 Inexpensive

MELBOURNE GENERAL CEMETERY

mgc.smct.org.au

A wander through this 100-acre historic cemetery is serene and quite beautiful. Significant sites include the Prime Ministers Garden, St Mary of the Cross Mausoleum and the Elvis Memorial Grotto. Take a night tour and visit the graves in the dead of night as Melbourne's bats fly overhead.

City ferries at Williamstown

➕ See map ▷ 93   ✉ College Crescent, Parkville   ☎ 9349 3014   ⏰ Daily 8–6   🚋 Tram 1, 6   ♿ Few   💲 Free. Night tour moderate

MONTSALVAT

montsalvat.com.au

This artists' colony was handcrafted between 1934 and the 1970s, using mud brick, stone, hewn timbers and slate building materials recycled from some of Melbourne's fine old buildings.

➕ See map ▷ 93   ✉ 7 Hillcrest Avenue, Eltham   ☎ 9439 7712   ⏰ Daily 9–5   🚆 To Eltham then take 582 bus   💲 Inexpensive

RAAF MUSEUM POINT COOK

airforce.gov.au/raafmuseum

Based at Point Cook, the birthplace of the Australian Flying Corps and the Royal Australian Air Force, this museum presents the history of the second-oldest air force in the world.

➕ See map ▷ 92   ✉ RAAF Base Williams, Point Cook Road, Point Cook   ☎ 8348 6040   ⏰ Tue–Fri 10–3, Sat–Sun 10–5. Interactive flying displays Tue, Thu, Sun 1   🚆 Werribee Park Shuttle daily to Point Cook   💲 Free/donations

WILLIAMSTOWN

This bayside suburb is best reached by the Westgate Bridge or by a ferry from Southbank and seaside St. Kilda. Shipping docks, moored yachts, boat chandlers and the restored World War II corvette HMAS *Castlemaine* all add to the maritime atmosphere. Walk along the Strand to take in the craft shops.

➕ See map ▷ 92   ✉ The Strand, The Marina   🍴 Many cafés and restaurants   🚆 Williamstown Beach   ⛴ Southbank

DANDENONG RANGES

The scenic Dandenongs have always been the favored summer recreation destination for many Melburnians.

Soaring mountain ash forests, glades of tree ferns and mountain streams are all part of the experience in the Dandenongs. The highest point is Mount Dandenong at 633m (2,076ft). Besides hiking and picnicking, there are magnificent gardens, art and craft shops, nurseries and tearooms to visit. Along the southeastern slopes, on the edge of Sherbrooke Forest, the narrow-gauge Puffing Billy Railway carries day-trippers from quaint Belgrave, in the foothills, to pretty Emerald Lake Park in the mountains.

William Ricketts Sanctuary, set in a 1.6ha (4-acre) wooded area, displays 200 half-hidden, kiln-fired, clay sculptures of Aboriginal figures, the work of the talented sculptor William Ricketts (1898–1993), who founded the sanctuary, nestled among mossy rocks and tree ferns. Follow the path around the tranquil setting and visit the log cabin Visual Display Centre to watch a short documentary.

HEALESVILLE SANCTUARY

One of Australia's most highly regarded wildlife parks, Healesville is set in the foothills of the scenic Yarra Valley.

Observe hundreds of native species, including kangaroos, emus, koalas, wombats, dingoes and platypuses, in surroundings as near natural as possible. You can learn about the animals from their keepers, as they go on their daily rounds. There are also walk-through aviaries, a wetlands walkway and a nocturnal house. See the working wildlife hospital where sick, injured and orphaned wildlife are cared for, and talk with the vets about native wildlife health. Learn about Australia's majestic birds of prey and parrots at the spectacular Spirits of the Sky show. Tales from Platypus Creek lets you get up close to platypuses. Both events are held daily.

THE BASICS

visitdandenongranges.com.au

Distance: 35km (22 miles) east of the city

Journey Time: 45 minutes

🚆 Ferntree Gully, then Bus 688

♿ Poor

Puffing Billy

puffingbilly.com.au

✉ Belgrave Station

☎ 9757 0700

🕐 Daily 10.30–2.30

✋ Expensive

THE BASICS

zoo.org.au/healesville

Distance: 60km (38 miles) northeast of the city

Journey Time: 1 hour

✉ Badger Creek Road, Healesville

☎ 1300 966 784

🕐 Daily 9–5

🍴 Cafés; picnic areas

🚆 Lilydale Station then Bus 685 to Healesville, then Bus 686

✋ Expensive

THE BASICS

visitgreatoceanroad.org.au
Distance: 243km
(150 miles)
Journey Time: 9 hours
🅸 Geelong and Great
Ocean Road Visitor Centre
✉ Princes Highway, Little
River ☎ 1800 755 611
❓ Bus tours from
Melbourne

GREAT OCEAN ROAD

Built by soldiers returned from World War I, and opened in 1932, the Great Ocean Road is one of the world's great scenic drives.

The journey from Torquay, southwest of Melbourne, to Warrnambool and beyond encompasses rain forests, seaside beach towns, cliff-edge roadways, forests and dramatic off-shore rock formations. Past Torquay and nearby Bells Beach (regarded as Australia's surfing capital) is the popular and quaint seaside town of Lorne, and the nearby beachside village Apollo Bay.

Near Port Campbell you encounter the famed Twelve Apostles, natural rock formations, weathered by the wind and water, standing in the ocean just offshore. Loch Ard Gorge, the site of a legendary shipwreck, can be reached by a walking trail. The Great Ocean Road is an excellent bus day tour, but could also be undertaken in a more leisurely way as a self-drive trip.

THE BASICS

visitphillipisland.com
Distance: 140km
(86 miles)
Journey Time: 2 hours
🅸 Phillip Island Visitor
Centre ✉ 895 Phillip
Island Road, Newhaven
☎ 1300 366 422
🕐 Penguin Parade every
night after sunset
🍴 Restaurants; picnic
areas
**Penguin Parade &
Koala Conservation
Centre**
penguins.org.au
☎ 5951 2800
💲 Moderate to expensive

PHILLIP ISLAND

On the island's Summerland Beach you can view a colony of little penguins every night at the Penguin Parade.

Spotlights illuminate these engaging birds as thousands of them return to their nesting burrows in the evening. There is commentary from an experienced ranger and a choice of viewing places, including an underground viewing window.

Bring warm clothing, as nights can be cold and the weather unpredictable. Phillip Island has a substantial waterbird population and there are elevated boardwalks through bush-land allowing good viewing opportunities.

At the Koala Conservation Centre, located on Phillip Island Tourist Road in Cowes, you can wander along treetop boardwalks and easily spot koalas, or walk the 1km (0.6-mile) track around the center, where there are signs pointing to koalas in trees. Look also for wallabies, echidnas and native birds.

WERRIBEE MANSION AND OPEN RANGE ZOO

This renovated old mansion stands on the banks of the Werribee River, a 30-minute drive from the city, on the way to Geelong.

An audio tour explores this imposing, 19th-century example of Australia's pastoral heritage. Constructed between 1874 and 1877, the Italianate mansion, with its 10ha (25 acres) of formal grounds, bluestone farm buildings and orchard, is the largest private residence ever built in Victoria. Next to the mansion, the Victoria State Rose Garden has over 5,000 rose bushes.

At the Open Range Zoo you can either stroll around the zoo at your own pace, or jump on a safari bus and drive around the grassy plains and sweeping river terraces. Giraffes, zebras, antelopes and hippos roam freely here. Walking tracks pass natural enclosures with cheetahs, monkeys and ostriches.

THE BASICS

parkweb.vic.gov.au/
explore/parks/werribee-
park
zoo.org.au/werribee
Distance: 29km (18 miles)
Journey Time: 30
minutes
☒ K Road, Werribee
☎ The Mansion: 8734
5100. Open Range Zoo:
9731 9600
🕐 The Mansion: daily
10–5. Victoria State Rose
Garden: daily 9–5. Open
Range Zoo: daily 9–5
🍽 Café, bistro and kiosk
💰 Zoo: expensive.
Mansion: inexpensive

YARRA VALLEY

Northeast of Melbourne, the Yarra River is very different to how it is in the city, and makes for a great day trip.

In the pretty town of Eltham, don't miss the artists' colony at Montsalvat (▷ 100). There's also the Diamond Valley Miniature Railway in Eltham Lower Park. At Yering, the Yarra Valley Dairy sells handmade cheeses.

There are hundreds of wineries in the cool-climate Yarra Valley and plenty of cellar doors to visit. Around 60 percent represent Chardonnay and Pinot Noir, and toward the northern end of the valley, you'll find Cabernet Sauvignon and Shiraz, too. Many other varieties are grown, including Sauvignon Blanc, Pinot Grigio and rosés.

Farther on is Healesville Sanctuary (▷ 101), with its native animal species, including the rarely seen platypus, in natural surroundings of bushland and wetlands. Many bus tours run to this district.

THE BASICS

visityarravalley.com.au
Distance: 52km (32
miles) northeast of
Melbourne
Journey Time: Allow a
full day to take in the sights
Yarra Valley Dairy
yvd.com.au
☒ McMeikans Road,
Yering
☎ 9739 0023

Shopping

A1 LEBANESE BAKERY

a1lebanesebakery.com.au

All the hard-to-get spices, oils and other exotic ingredients are here at this Mediterranean grocer, plus breads, pizzas and sweets in the bakery.

🔳 Off map 🖂 643 Sydney Road, Brunswick ☎ 9386 0440 🕐 Mon–Wed & Sun 7–7, Thu–Sat 7am–9pm 🚊 Tram 19

ARMADALE ANTIQUE CENTRE

armadaleantiquecentre.com.au

Quality antiques and collectibles are sold here. Find collectibles ranging from prints and maps to glass and silver.

🔳 Off map 🖂 1147 High Street, Armadale ☎ 9822 7788 🕐 Daily 10–5 🚊 Tram 6

CAMBERWELL SUNDAY MARKET

camberwellsundaymarket.org

Several hundred stallholders sell a wide assortment of bric-a-brac at this enormous flea market.

🔳 Off map 🖂 Station Street, Camberwell 🕐 Sun 6.30am–12.30pm 🚊 Tram 70, 72, 75

DE BORTOLI WINERY

debortoliyarra.com.au

This is one of the best wineries and restaurants in the Yarra Valley, with fantastic views. Sample, then buy your wines, pick up some great cheeses and dine on the excellent northern Italian food based on local produce. You need a car to get here.

🔳 Off map 🖂 58 Pinnacle Lane, Dixons Creek ☎ 5965 2271 🕐 Cellar door: daily 10–5

NATIONAL WOOL MUSEUM SHOP

geelongaustralia.com.au/nwm

An excellent range of wool products is for sale at Australia's comprehensive wool museum, in a century-old wool store with displays and hands-on exhibits highlighting all facets of this industry.

🔳 Off map 🖂 26 Moorabool Street, Geelong ☎ 5272 4701 🕐 Daily 9–5

POST INDUSTRIAL DESIGN

postindustrialdesign.com.au

Way out west, Post Industrial Design is worth a visit to check out the bespoke art and design and quirky gifts. Stay a while at in-house café "Pod" for coffee, healthy breakfasts and hearty lunches.

🔳 Off map 🖂 638 Barkly Street, West Footscray ☎ 9362 7703 🕐 Tue–Sat 9–5, Sun 9–3 🚊 Tram 19

ST. KILDA ESPLANADE MARKET

stkildaesplanademarket.com.au

Original works made by stallholders at this popular Sunday arts and crafts market draw shoppers from far and wide. Pick up something to eat from the "Flavours of the World" foodie section.

🔳 Off map 🖂 The Upper Esplanade, St. Kilda 🕐 Sun 10–4 🚊 Tram 16, 96

TARRAWARRA WINERY

tarrawarra.com.au

The subterranean cellar door is a must-visit—an architectural wonder cut into a hillside and a great space to taste TarraWarra's signature Chardonnay and Pinot Noir. The on-site restaurant has stunning views.

🔳 Off map 🖂 311 Healesville–Yarra Glen Road ☎ 5957 3511 🕐 Cellar door: Tue–Sun 11–5

MEGA MALLS

A trip to Melbourne's major suburban shopping centers finds cinemas, restaurants and free entertainment. Try the Chadstone Shopping Centre (🖂 1341 Dandenong Road, Chadstone 🕐 Mon–Wed, 9–5.30, Thu–Sat 9–9, Sun 10–7, 🚇 Hughsdale, then 15-min walk).

Entertainment and Nightlife

BACK ALLEY SALLY'S

backalleysallys.com.au

Heaps of booths line one brick wall and heaps of booze line the other at this upstairs laneway bar in Footscray. Pizzas come courtesy of Slice Girls West.

➕ Off map ✉ 4 Yewers Street ☎ 9689 6260 🕐 Mon–Wed 5–11pm, Thu 4pm–midnight, Fri & Sat noon–midnight, Sun 1–10pm 🚆 Footscray

BALLOONMAN

balloonman.com.au

View Melbourne from a hot-air balloon followed by a champagne breakfast. Fly over the MCG, Westgate Bridge and past the Eureka Tower.

➕ Off map ✉ 10 Bond Street, Abbotsford ☎ 1800 468 247 🕐 Daily at dawn

BRUNSWICK JAZZLAB

jazzlab.club

Every night of the week, this New York-style club with superb acoustics plays host to local and international jazz acts.

➕ Off map ✉ 27 Leslie Street, Brunswick ☎ 9388 1999 🕐 Daily for shows 🚆 Brunswick 🚋 Tram 19

FLEMINGTON RACECOURSE

flemington.com.au

Huge crowds head to Flemington racecourse for the Melbourne Cup and a regular program of race days year-round.

➕ Off map ✉ 448 Epsom Road, Flemington ☎ 1300 727 575 🚋 Tram 57

MOONRAKER DOLPHIN SWIMS

moonrakercharters.com.au

On boat tours in pristine Port Phillip Bay, you may choose to swim with the wild bottlenose dolphins or simply sightsee in comfort.

➕ Off map ✉ Esplanade Road, Sorrento ☎ 5984 4211 🕐 Tours on demand

MRS HOPPER

mrs-hopper.com.au

The cocktail front bar of Sri Lankan restaurant Araliya is the place to enjoy a house cocktail accompanied by bite-size hoppers (bowl-shaped crepes) filled with your choice of meat, fish or veggies.

➕ Off map ✉ 157 Fitzroy Street, St. Kilda ☎ 0421 611 406 🕐 Tue–Thu 5pm–late, Fri–Sun noon–late 🚋 Tram 3, 16, 96

MR WEST

mrwest.com.au

Perched upstairs above its own bottle shop in Footscray's mall, Mr West has a huge craft beer tap list on a blackboard at its long bar, plus a heap of wines and cocktails to choose from, too. The industrial space is filled with comfy booths and communal tables.

➕ Off map ✉ 106 Nicholson Street, Footscray ☎ No phone 🕐 Wed–Fri 4pm–late, Sat & Sun 1pm–late 🚆 Footscray

PRINCE BANDROOM

princebandroom.com.au

Inside the Prince of Wales hotel, for over 60 years the bandroom has been a hot-spot venue for top musicians. The public bar is open late and has live music too.

➕ Off map ✉ 29 Fitzroy Street, St. Kilda ☎ 9536 1168 🕐 Bar: daily lunchtime; Bandroom: daily 8pm–late 🚋 Tram 12, 16, 96

ST. KILDA SEA BATHS

stkildaseabaths.com.au

Near St. Kilda Pier, the complex houses a 25m (82 ft) seawater public pool, gym and spa, plus cafés and restaurants.

➕ Off map ✉ 10–18 Jacka Boulevard, St. Kilda ☎ 9525 4888 🕐 Mon–Thu 5am–11pm, Fri 5am–10pm, Sat 7am–8pm, Sun 8–8 🚋 Tram 16, 96

Where to Eat

PRICES
Prices are approximate, based on a 3-course meal for one person. $ A$25–A$45 $$ A$46–A$75 $$$ A$76–A$120

ATTICA ($$$)

attica.com.au

Save your cash (almost AU$300) for the foodie experience of a lifetime. This is relaxed fine dining where you will marvel at the inventive use of Australian ingredients. Made top 50 in the World's Best Restaurants in 2018.

⊞ Off map ✉ 74 Glen Eira Road, Ripponlea ☎ 9530 0111 ⏰ Dinner Tue–Sat; no walk-ins; reserve 3 months in advance 🚉 Sandringham

DONOVANS ($$$)

donovanshouse.com.au

A Melbourne favorite, in a good beachside location, serves Mediterranean dishes with a modern twist. Seasonal produce and Victorian wines feature.

⊞ Off map ✉ 40 Jacka Boulevard, St. Kilda ☎ 9534 8221 ⏰ Lunch & dinner daily 🚋 Tram 16, 96

HARLEY & ROSE ($)

harleyandrose.net.au

A pizzeria that's worth traveling to WeFo for. Eat in or take them outside to the communal tables for a mouthwatering tasting session with your mates.

⊞ Off map ✉ 572 Barkly Street, West Footscray ☎ 8320 0325 ⏰ Tue–Fri 4pm–late, Sat & Sun 11.30am–late 🚉 West Footscray

THE HEALESVILLE HOTEL ($$)

healesvillehotel.com.au

This country pub has a contemporary seasonal menu and an interesting wine list. Go for the garden bbq.

⊞ Off map ✉ 256 Maroondah Highway, Healesville ☎ 5962 4002 ⏰ Lunch and dinner daily

HORN PLEASE ($$)

hornplease.com.au

A feast for your eyes and for your belly, Horn Please dishes up an innovative take on Indian street food and curries in a majestic restaurant with soaring ceilings and colorful art.

⊞ Off map ✉ 167 St. Georges Road, Fitzroy North ☎ 9497 8101 ⏰ Sun–Wed 6–9pm, Thu–Sat 6pm–late 🚋 Tram 11

LAKSA KING ($)

laksaking.com.au

Laksa never tasted better outside of Malaysia. Squeeze in at communal tables in this sprawling restaurant, tuck into spicy curry *laksa*, and find out why this place is called the king.

⊞ Off map ✉ 6–12 Pin Oak Crescent, Flemington ☎ 9372 6383 ⏰ Daily 11.30–3, 5–10pm (10.30pm Fri & Sat) 🚉 Newmarket (Flemington) 🚋 Tram 57

SKY HIGH RESTAURANT ($$)

skyhighmtdandenong.com.au

Contemporary Australian dining with sensational observatory views of the Mornington Peninsula to Port Phillip Bay.

⊞ Off map ✉ 26 Observatory Road, Mount Dandenong ☎ 9751 0443 ⏰ Daily 9.15am–10.30am, noon–4, 6–10pm

VUE GRAND HOTEL ($$)

vuegrand.com.au

Choose from a menu of fine cuisine and a great craft beer and wine list in the majestic Grand Dining Room, or opt for a more casual dinner in the bar.

⊞ Off map ✉ 46 Hesse Street, Queenscliff ☎ 5258 1544 ⏰ Dinner Wed–Sat; reservations essential

There are many fabulous places to stay in Melbourne, from budget to boutique. Enjoy your stay in hotel rooms adorned with art, five-star fancy penthouses, minimalist apartments and even a home away from home in a residential Victorian terrace.

Introduction

Take your pick from a range of areas to stay, in all types of accommodations. You may prefer the quieter suburbs to the buzz of central Melbourne.

A Wide Choice

Melbourne has plenty of accommodations options. At the upper end there's the luxurious QT Melbourne (▷ 112) in the city and South Yarra's The Olsen (▷ 112), and the less expensive, classy boutique The Prince (▷ 111) at St. Kilda. At the lower end are the comfortable rooms at The Jasper (▷ 109) and the convenient Hotel Claremont (▷ 109). There are also many economical, self-catering apartments and reasonably priced guesthouses. Bed-and-breakfasts are numerous, especially in outer suburbs and rural areas close to the city.

Where to Stay

Melbourne's major hotel areas are located around the city center, East Melbourne and Southbank. South Yarra and St. Kilda play host to fabulous art and boutique hotels.

Get a Bargain

It's worth looking on the Internet for special deals, for both advance reservations and last-minute rate reductions. But be aware that there are popular times of the year, such as around Melbourne Cup time (early November) and the Grand Prix (mid-March), when hotels are often fully booked, so advance reservations really are essential.

STAY AT THE AIRPORT

Although Melbourne's CBD is only 22km (14 miles) from the international airport, there are times when a stay at an airport hotel is necessary. There are three good options, one in each of the price ranges: budget, mid-range and luxury. Ibis Budget Melbourne Airport (☎ 8336 1811) is a good budget option; Holiday Inn Melbourne Airport offers mid-range value (☎ 9933 5111); ParkRoyal Melbourne Airport (☎ 8347 2000) is the top-end choice.

Budget Hotels

169 DRUMMOND STREET

169drummond.com.au

This home-away-from-home bed-and-breakfast is housed in a 19th-century terrace close to the shops and restaurants of Lygon Street and has king, queen and twin rooms, laundry facilities and a garden area.

➕ F2 ✉ 169 Drummond Street, Carlton ☎ 9663 3081 🚋 Tram 1, 3, 5, 6, 16, 64, 67, 72

ATLANTIS HOTEL

atlantishotel.com.au

This stylish hotel has suites with great views over the city and Victoria Harbour. Rooms are spacious and comfortable, there's an indoor swimming pool, and continental breakfast is included.

➕ B5 ✉ 300 Spencer Street ☎ 9600 2900 🚋 Tram 86

CITY LIMITS

citylimits.com.au

On the edge of Chinatown, City Limits has 32 serviced studio apartments, which mostly accommodate up to two people. Functional rooms have comfortable beds, clean bathrooms and complimentary continental breakfast.

➕ G4 ✉ 20–22 Little Bourke Street ☎ 9662 2544 🚋 Tram 86, 96

HOTEL CLAREMONT GUESTHOUSE

hotelclaremont.com

The Claremont is a great-value, convenient guesthouse with bright rooms. Enjoy free breakfast in the breakfast room, a guest lounge and laundry facilities.

➕ Off map ✉ 189 Toorak Road, South Yarra ☎ 9826 8000 🚉 South Yarra 🚋 Tram 58, 78

JASPER HOTEL

jasperhotel.com.au

Each level of the Jasper Hotel reflects a different color of the jasper gem. The hotel offers a good range of reasonably priced accommodations, plus a fitness center, an indoor pool and café.

➕ D4 ✉ 489 Elizabeth Street ☎ 8327 2777 🚋 City Circle Tram

SPACE HOTEL

spacehotel.com.au

Facilities at this comfortable hotel with dorms, family and private rooms, include a gym, movie room, Internet café, shared kitchen and a rooftop sundeck with spa.

➕ E4 ✉ 380 Russell Street ☎ 9662 3888 🚋 Tram 24, 30, 35

TOLARNO HOTEL

tolarnohotel.com.au

This boutique hotel is in a heritage building in the heart of St. Kilda. All rooms are en suite and feature original artwork. View the fabulous art collection and dine on classic European fare at the hotel restaurant. Was once the private residence of Melbourne artist Mirka Mora.

➕ Off map ✉ 42 Fitzroy Street, St. Kilda ☎ 9537 0200 🚋 Tram 3A, 16, 96

VIBE CARLTON

vibehotels.com/hotel/carlton-melbourne

Handy if you're visiting the zoo, Vibe has spacious rooms with park or outdoor pool views and all the mod cons. There's an on-site restaurant and for a bit extra full breakfast is included.

➕ Off map ✉ 441 Royal Parade, Parkville ☎ 13 84 23 🚋 Tram 19

Mid-Range Hotels

ADINA APARTMENT HOTEL

adinahotels.com

Located right at the heart of Melbourne's attractions, the Adina has 1- and 2-bedroom apartments, a warehouse loft and penthouse apartments. There are well-maintained kitchens, a gym and on-site parking. No restaurant, but you're spoilt for choice with fabulous restaurants on your doorstep.

✚ G6 ✉ 88 Flinders Street ☎ 8663 0000 🚋 City Circle Tram

THE BLACKMAN

artserieshotels.com.au/blackman

What better place to lay your head than in a bed with Charles Blackman's dreamlike paintings on the walls around you? Settle into open-plan suites with top-notch amenities and balconies with views of Albert Park Lake. There's a couple of dining options, bike hire and complimentary pram hire.

✚ G12 ✉ 452 St. Kilda Road ☎ 9039 1444 🚋 Tram 3, 5, 6, 16, 64, 67, 72

BROOKLYN ARTS HOTEL

brooklynartshotel.com.au

On a residential street in Fitzroy, this charming Victorian terrace is run by Sydney film director Maggie Fooke. The quirky old house has seven rooms, two of which have balconies and en suites. It's an artist's retreat of sorts, coupled with the grandeur of old. There's a gorgeous garden to relax in and continental breakfast is included.

✚ H4 ✉ 48–50 George Street, Fitzroy ☎ 9419 9328 🚋 Tram 11

THE COMO

accorhotels.com

This top hotel, located in the vibrant heart of South Yarra, has studios and suites, great food, a gymnasium, sauna and pool. Bedrooms are sleek and stylish, and black-marble bathrooms have Japanese-style baths, perfect for a soak.

✚ Off map ✉ 630 Chapel Street, South Yarra ☎ 9825 2222 🚋 Tram 58, 78

COPPERSMITH HOTEL

coppersmithhotel.com.au

A residential boutique hotel with bar and bistro, the Coppersmith has refined rooms with en-suite bathrooms and your very own coffee machine. You can customize your mini bar and they'll give you a myki card to top up to get your expeditions started.

✚ E12 ✉ 435 Clarendon Street, South Melbourne ☎ 8696 7777 🚋 Tram 1, 12, 96

COSMOPOLITAN HOTEL

cosmopolitanhotel.com.au

The Cosmopolitan is a modern boutique hotel in the heart of St. Kilda. Rooms include doubles through to 2-bedroom apartments. There's a café onsite and free parking.

✚ Off map ✉ 2–8 Carlisle Street, St. Kilda ☎ 8598 6700 🚋 Tram 16, 96

CROSSLEY HOTEL

crossleyhotel.com.au

The Crossley offers both contemporary hotel rooms and self-contained apartments with en-suite bathrooms, comfy beds and some with balconies. There's a dedicated breakfast room, which has complimentary fresh fruit, coffee and tea all day, plus a late-night taqueria in the basement.

✚ F5 ✉ 51 Little Bourke Street ☎ 9639 1639 🚋 City Circle Tram

THE CULLEN

artserieshotels.com.au/cullen

Adam Cullen's original artworks adorn the walls of this boutique hotel. Accommodations are spacious and rooms at the top have fabulous views of the city. Two great restaurants are on the first floor of the hotel—try comfort food at Gramercy Social or dumplings at HuTong Dumpling Bar.

➕ Off map ✉ 164 Commercial Road, Prahran ☎ 9098 1555 🚋 Tram 72

THE LARWILL STUDIO

artserieshotels.com.au/larwill

Cheer yourself up with a stay at the Larwill where rooms and spaces are adorned with the works of Victorian expressionist artist David Larwell. The 96 airy rooms feature comfy beds and yoga mats, plus there's an on-site gym and restaurant, and art tours.

➕ Off map ✉ 48 Flemington Road, Parkville ☎ 9032 9111 🚋 Tram 58, 59

PARKVIEW ST. KILDA ROAD HOTEL

viewhotels.com.au

Located not far from the city, Parkview has well-appointed rooms, a restaurant and bar, and a roof-top spa and sauna. Some terrific city and park views.

➕ Off map ✉ 562 St. Kilda Road ☎ 9529 8888 🚋 Tram 3, 16, 96

THE PRINCE

theprince.com.au

Nothing quite matches a stay at this particularly stylish and elegant boutique hotel. Rooms are clean and crisp, and some suites have bay-view balconies. There's also a wellness center with spa treatments.

➕ Off map ✉ 2 Acland Street, St. Kilda ☎ 9536 1111 🚋 Tram 3, 16, 96

ROYCE HOTEL

roycehotel.com.au

A grand sweeping staircase and soaring ceilings in the lobby greet guests at this elegant hotel. Understated rooms have modern furniture and Italian-marble bathrooms, and breakfast is served in the Modern Australian-inspired Dish Restaurant. Head to the Amberoom lounge bar for a nightcap before bed.

➕ G11 ✉ 379 St. Kilda Road ☎ 9677 9900 🚋 Tram 3, 5, 6, 16, 58, 64, 67, 72

STAMFORD PLAZA

stamford.com.au/spm

Rooms at the Stamford range from studios with spa baths to suites with full kitchens. There's a fabulous indoor/outdoor rooftop pool and spa area with a retractable roof, plus an on-site restaurant.

➕ F5 ✉ 111 Little Collins Street ☎ 9659 1000 🚋 Tram 11, 12, 48, 109

TREASURY ON COLLINS

treasuryoncollins.com.au

Back in 1876 this heritage-listed apartment-hotel used to be The Bank of Australasia. Now it's a boutique space offering a loft, 1- and 2-bedroom apartments as well as a variety of suites. Relax in the Treasured Guest Lounge or watch Netflix for free in your room.

➕ D6 ✉ 394 Collins Street ☎ 8535 8535 🚋 City Circle Tram

APARTMENTS

If you want to self-cater, Melbourne has many serviced apartment-style hotels that are large enough for families or small groups. They have from one to three bedrooms, with separate dining areas and kitchens or kitchenettes. A quick Internet search reveals just how many.

Luxury Hotels

ADELPHI
adelphi.com.au

If you love a rooftop pool, the Adelphi's is a stunner—it hangs over the edge of the building. With a cozy 34 rooms all decorated to the hilt, and a free (non-alcoholic) mini bar, it's no wonder this boutique hotel is winning awards.

 F6 ✉ 187 Flinders Lane ☎ 8080 8888 🚋 City Circle Tram

CROWN PROMENADE
crownpromenade.com.au

The ultimate in luxury, this hotel has a casino, world-class health center, classy shopping centers and stylish waterfront restaurants at its doorstep. Stay in contemporary rooms or studios with floor-to-ceiling windows.

E7 ✉ Southbank ☎ 9292 6688 🚉 Flinders Street 🚋 Tram 12, 58, 96, 109

GRAND HYATT MELBOURNE
melbourne.grand.hyatt.com

One of Melbourne's best hotels, the Grand Hyatt has very good restaurants, a health and fitness center, business facilities and exclusive boutiques. Rooms have Yarra River or city views.

F6 ✉ 123 Collins Street ☎ 9657 1234 🚋 City Circle Tram

HOTEL WINDSOR
thehotelwindsor.com.au

One of the world's finest hotels and certainly Australia's grandest and most steeped in history, this luxury hotel offers fine service and a sense of style. If you don't stay here, it's worth dropping in for afternoon tea.

G5 ✉ 111 Spring Street ☎ 9633 6000 🚋 City Circle Tram

INTERCONTINENTAL MELBOURNE RIALTO
melbourne.intercontinental.com

Stylish luxury hotel in a heritage-listed building, with top service, a great location, bars, a brasserie and a heated rooftop pool and sauna.

D7 ✉ 495 Collins Street ☎ 8627 1400 🚋 City Circle Tram

LANGHAM HOTEL
langhamhotels.com.au

Go all out and get your own private terrace overlooking the Melbourne skyline. Rooms are elegant and facilities include a business center, health club and a heated pool.

E7 ✉ 1 Southgate Avenue (short walk from city center) ☎ 8696 8888 🚋 City Circle Tram

THE OLSEN
artserieshotels.com.au/olsen

Another from the Art Series Group, this version's rooms display art by traditional landscape artist Dr John Olsen. Refined rooms are bathed in natural light and breakfasts are served in the upscale Spoonbill Restaurant.

Off map ✉ 637–641 Chapel Street, South Yarra ☎ 9040 1222 🚉 South Yarra 🚋 Tram 58, 78

QT MELBOURNE
qthotelsandresorts.com/melbourne

Housed in an industrial-chic space with arty rooms to match, this is no ordinary hotel. Head to the Pascale Bar & Grill for breakfast or dinner or enjoy cocktails from the spectacular roof-top bar.

F5 ✉ 6133 Russell Street ☎ 8636 8800 🚋 Tram 86, 96

The more you plan your trip, the more you'll get out of your time in Melbourne, which has so much to offer. These pages of travel advice and facts will give you insider knowledge of the city.

Planning Ahead

When to Go

Summer is the busiest and hottest time to visit Melbourne, when festivals and celebrations are happening all over the city, plus it's a good time for a trip to the beach or walks in Melbourne's many beautiful parks and gardens. Be sure to reserve accommodations in advance in busy periods.

TIME

Melbourne is 11 hours ahead of London, 16 hours ahead of New York City and 19 ahead of Los Angeles.

AVERAGE DAILY MAXIMUM TEMPERATURES

JAN	FEB	MAR	APR	MAY	JUN	JUL	AUG	SEP	OCT	NOV	DEC
79°F	79°F	75°F	68°F	63°F	57°F	55°F	59°F	63°F	68°F	72°F	75°F
26°C	26°C	24°C	20°C	17°C	14°C	13°C	15°C	17°C	20°C	22°C	24°C

Melbourne's weather changes frequently—always carry an umbrella, even if it doesn't look like rain. The city enjoys a generally temperate climate.

Spring (September–November) is cool to mild, with average highs of 20°C and average lows of 10°C, perfect for being out and about.

Summer (December–February) can be warm to hot, and many locals head for the beaches.

Autumn (March–May) is mild—good weather for parks and gardens.

Winter (June–August) can be wet and cold.

WHAT'S ON

January *Cricket matches:* At Melbourne Cricket Ground. *Australian Open Tennis:* The classic tournament is at Melbourne Park. *Midsumma Festival:* Annual celebration of gay culture.

February *Chinese New Year:* Two weeks of festivities. *White Night:* Melbourne comes alive with light and sound.

March *Formula 1 Australian Grand Prix:* Albert Park. *The Moomba Festival:* A Melbourne institution with parades and exhibitions. *Melbourne Food and Wine Festival:* Sample Australia's best food and wines here. *Melbourne Queer Film Festival:* Oldest LGBT+ film festival in the country. *Melbourne International Flower and Garden Show:* Indoor exhibition.

April *Melbourne International Comedy Festival:* One of the largest comedy festivals in the world. *Rip Curl Pro Classic:* Australia's most prestigious surfing event.

August *Melbourne International Film Festival:* A showcase for top local and international movies.

September *Australian Rules Grand Final:* The top teams compete. *Royal Melbourne Show:* Food, animals, events, art and crafts.

October *Italian Festival:* Piazza Italia.

October/November *Melbourne Cup and Spring Racing Carnival:* The Melbourne Cup is the highlight of these prestigious races. *Melbourne Festival:* Art exhibitions, concerts, plays and dance performances.

December *New Year's Eve:* Fireworks and partying along the Yarra River.

Melbourne Online

bom.gov.au
The national bureau of meteorology, with comprehensive weather information and forecasts.

broadsheet.com.au/melbourne
Up-to-date coverage of what's happening in Melbourne, covering all things eating, drinking and shopping.

smartraveller.com.au
The Australian Government travel advisory service. As well as travel alerts, the site allows you to register your particulars so that you can be contacted in an emergency. It links to sites providing information on travel insurance, health insurance and cheap airline flights.

starobserver.com.au
LGBT+ news site, covering the whole of Australia.

theage.com.au
The Age is Melbourne's major daily newspaper, with coverage of the latest local, national and world news stories, as well as sections on breaking news and business, travel, technology and entertainment.

timeout.com/melbourne/lgbt
Lists LGBT+ events, bars and clubs in Melbourne.

visitmelbourne.com
Melbourne's official travel and accommodations website, with things to do, route planners, road maps and more.

whatson.melbourne.vic.gov.au
Melbourne's government website for tourists has up-to-date, comprehensive information on city attractions, events, guided tours, shopping, accommodations, eating out and lots more.

Getting There

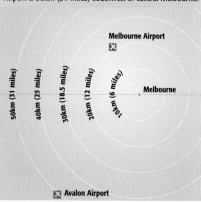

TASMANIA

WHAT TO PACK

● In summer (December–February) the temperature averages 25°C (77°F) and has been known to hit a whopping 45°C (113°F). Take cotton clothing, a broadbrimmed hat, sunscreen, sunglasses and other summer-weight items, plus an umbrella.
● In winter (June–August) take a raincoat and/or medium-weight coat, plus clothing suitable for an average 13°C (55°F).

BEFORE YOU GO

● All foreign visitors need a valid passport and an ETA (Electronic Travel Authority). It is fully electronic and is available through travel agents.
● A Tourist ETA is valid for one year (or until the expiry date of your passport, if less), allows for multiple entry and will allow you to stay for a total of three months. Australia does not allow entry if your passport expires within six months of your entry date.
● Vaccination certificates are not normally required, unless you have traveled to an infected country within the previous 14 days.

AIRPORTS

Melbourne Airport is 22km (14 miles) northwest of Melbourne's Central Business District (CBD). Avalon Airport is 50km (31 miles) southwest of central Melbourne.

ARRIVING BY AIR

Melbourne Airport (melbourneairport.com.au) at Tullamarine, to the northwest of the city, is the main point of entry for overseas visitors on direct flights. The airport also handles the majority of domestic passenger arrivals. There are taxis and inexpensive bus services, including Skybus (tel 1300 759 287, skybus.com.au), that travel into the city, as well as a variety of car rental outlets. A second airport, southwest of the city, Avalon Airport, serves domestic carrier JetStar's flights, and Sita Coaches (tel 9689 7999) meet flights and take 50 minutes to Melbourne CBD.

ARRIVING BY SEA

Not the most common means by which to arrive in Melbourne, but the city is an increasingly popular port for cruise liners. Melbourne's Station Pier, 4km (2.5 miles) from the city, serves cruise ships as well as being the dock of the *Spirit of Tasmania* (tel 1800 634 906, spiritoftasmania.com.au), the car and passenger ferry service between Melbourne and Devonport in Tasmania. A tram runs to and

from the pier to Collins Street in the city about every 15 minutes.

ARRIVING BY BUS

Bus travel can be more expensive than flying, but buses are nevertheless one of the best ways to see more of Australia and Victoria on your way to Melbourne. Country and interstate buses pick up and depart from Southern Cross Station. Day and overnight buses arrive each day from Adelaide and Sydney and usually take between 11 and 12 hours. The main interstate carrier is Greyhound Australia (tel 1300 473 946, greyhound.com.au).

ARRIVING BY TRAIN

Country and interstate trains (tel 1800 800 007, vline.com.au) travel to and around Victoria and offer a comfortable, if slower, way to see the state and other parts of Australia. Vline trains arrive at Southern Cross Station, part of the metropolitan train system's underground City Loop service. Countrylink XPT train services (tel 13 22 32, nswtrainlink.info) from Sydney to Melbourne take around 10–11 hours.

ARRIVING BY CAR

Car rental is relatively inexpensive in Australia and is a popular way for families to save money on interstate travel. The main highways between cities are excellent. Melbourne and larger regional centers have several car rental firms, offering a variety of vehicles and deals. You must be at least 21 years old, and you can pay additional fees to have the insurance excess waived. The main rental companies are Avis, Budget, Europcar, Hertz and Thrifty. Remember there are great distances involved in driving between Australian state capitals and to the many isolated attractions, so good planning is essential for a successful driving holiday. Driving in outback locations requires extra precautions and good driving skills. Check the Australian Automobile Association (aaa.asn.au) for more details.

CUSTOMS REGULATIONS

● Visitors aged 18 or over may bring in 25g cigarettes or 25g of tobacco or cigars; 2.25l of alcoholic spirits; plus other dutiable goods to the value of A$900 per person.
● There is no limit on money imported for personal use, although amounts in excess of A$10,000 or its equivalent must be declared on arrival.
● The smuggling of all drugs is treated harshly in Australia, and the importing of firearms and items such as ivory or other products from endangered species is illegal or restricted.

EMERGENCY TELEPHONE NUMBERS

Police, Ambulance, Fire
☎ 000 (24 hours)
Calls are free.

POLICE

The non-emergency police number is ☎ 9247 6666.

CONSULATES

● **Spain** ✉ 146 Elgin Street, Carlton ☎ 9347 1966
● **UK** ✉ Level 17, 90 Collins Street ☎ 9652 1600
● **US** ✉ 553 St. Kilda Road ☎ 9526 5900

Getting Around

● Myki cards allow for travel on trams, trains and buses. Three fare zones apply. There's a Free Tram Zone in the CBD that's clearly marked at each tram stop. Zone 1 covers inner Melbourne and Zone 2 outer Melbourne. Check out ptv.vic.gov.au/tickets/zones/ for more information.

● A two-hour full fare in Zone 1 costs up to A$4.30, daily full fare up to A$8.60. Go to ptv.vic.gov.au/tickets/ for up-to-date fare information.

● Myki cards can be bought at the airport, rail and bus stations, and at retail outlets displaying the myki sign. If in doubt call Public Transport Victoria on 1800 800 007.

● Melbourne is unforgiving when it comes to not having a myki card—fines are on-the-spot.

TRAMS AND LIGHT RAIL

Melbourne's excellent public transportation system is centered around its tram and light rail system. Ticketing is by touch card and a myki Explorer pack is just the thing for visitors (ptv.vic.gov.au/tickets/myki). Principal services operate from Swanston and Elizabeth streets (north and south); Flinders, Collins and Bourke streets and Batman Avenue (east and west). Trams operate between 5am and midnight weeknights and main routes all night on weekends.

The distinctive burgundy and gold free City Circle Trams run in both directions around the entire city center, at 12-minute intervals, from 10am to 6pm Sun–Wed and from 10am to 9pm Thu–Sat.

AIRPORT BUS

Skybus runs to Melbourne Airport, around the clock, daily. Drop-offs and pick-ups are available at city hotels, Southern Cross Bus Station and across the city, and at some regional centers. Cost is A$18 for adults and accompanied kids ride free (tel 1300 759 287).

BUSES

Melbourne's buses vary in color, depending on the company. Skybus (skybus.com.au) runs between Melbourne Airport and the city terminus. Privately run hop-on, hop-off buses take passengers around the main sights.

There are no specific bus terminals for suburban buses. Catch them at designated stops. Buy a myki card before you board.

Nightrider Buses can take you home safely on Saturday or Sunday mornings. They head for various suburban destinations every 30 to 60 minutes, picking up at designated stops, including those close to the major nightlife venues.

CAR RENTAL

Renting a car may be necessary for some of the out-of-town trips within this book. You must be over 21. Compulsory third-party insurance is included in rental prices, which are on average

A\$70–A\$90 per day. Overseas visitors require an international driving license.

Major Melbourne car rental companies are: Avis (tel 136 333); Budget (tel 1300 362 848); and Hertz (tel 133 039).

Full details of Australia's road rules are available from the Australian Automobile Association in Canberra (aaa.asn.au).

FERRIES

Ferries run from Southgate and from World Trade Centre wharves. These are primarily for tours but a ferry runs to Williamstown, from Southbank and St. Kilda, as public transportation. Buy tickets directly from the operators.

TAXIS

Taxis are meter-operated, yellow and clearly marked with a "Taxi" sign on top of the vehicle. The basic charge is around A\$4–A\$6 and the remainder of the fare is calculated based on time and distance (from A\$1.60 per km).

Main operators include 13 Cabs (tel 132 227) and Silver Top (tel 131 008). Ask for a taxi that can take a wheelchair if you need one.

TRAINS

Melbourne's inner-city rail lines include the City Loop (Parliament, Melbourne Central, Flagstaff Gardens, Southern Cross Station and Flinders Street Station).

Flinders Street Station is the main suburban rail terminus. Buy a myki card from booths or machines, and enter platforms via the automatic barriers. Trains operate 5am–midnight weeknights and all night weekends on major routes.

BICYCLES

Melbourne Bike Share provides locals and tourists with blue bikes and helmets to get around the city's many cycle lanes. There are lots of bike-share stations around the CBD where you can pick up and drop off a bike. Subscribe online at melbournebikeshare.com.au.

ETIQUETTE

● Smoking is prohibited on public transportation (including all internal flights and inside airport terminals), in bars, restaurants, cinemas, theaters, shops and shopping centers.
● There's no mandatory tipping in Melbourne. In restaurants and bars a 10 percent GST (goods and services) tax is included in your bill. However, it is commonplace, and appreciated, to leave a little extra for good waiting service.

STUDENT TRAVELERS

● International Student Identity Cards are not usually recognized by cinemas, theaters or public transportation authorities.
● There are many backpackers' lodges, YHA establishments and hostels in Melbourne (all busy in summer). YHA cardholders may obtain discounts.

TRAVEL INSURANCE

Ensure you have the appropriate insurance cover before departure.

NEED TO KNOW GETTING AROUND

Essential Facts

OPENING HOURS

● Shops: in the city center generally Mon–Thu 10–6, Fri 10–9, Sat–Sun 10–6. Suburban hours vary; corner shops often open daily 8–8 or later.
● Banks: Mon–Thu 9.30–4, Fri 9.30–5. City head-office banks open Mon–Fri 8.15–5.
● Museums and galleries: generally daily 10–5. Some close on one day of the week and hours may vary from day to day.

MONEY

The Australian unit of currency is the Australian dollar (A$), comprising 100 cents. Banknotes come in A$100, A$50, A$20, A$10 and A$5 denominations. Coins come in 5¢, 10¢, 20¢ and 50¢ (silver), and A$1 and A$2 (gold colored).

ELECTRICITY

● The electricity supply in Australia is 240 volts AC. Three-flat-pin plugs are the standard but are not the same as in the UK and adaptors are needed.
● Hotels provide standard 110-volt and 240-volt shaver sockets.

GOODS & SERVICES TAX (GST)

A 10 percent GST applies to all goods and services. The charge is added to bills.

INTERNATIONAL NEWSAGENTS

UK and US newspapers, as well as many foreign-language papers, are available from larger newsagents around the city center.

MAGAZINES

Beat magazine (beat.com.au) is Melbourne's gig guide; *Timeout Melbourne* (timeout.com/melbourne) is the city's entertainment guide.

MEDICAL TREATMENT

● Doctors and dentists are readily available and there are many medical centers where appointments are not necessary.
● Hotels will help you locate a doctor.
● Medical, dental and ambulance services are excellent, but costly.
● British, New Zealand and some other nationals are entitled to "immediate necessary treatment" under a reciprocal agreement but health insurance is still advisable. Dental services are not included.

MEDICINES

Visitors are permitted to bring prescribed medication in reasonable amounts. Remember to bring your prescription and leave medications in their original containers to avoid problems at customs. Most prescription drugs are widely available here. No vaccinations are required, unless you're entering from South America or Africa, when you need proof of yellow fever vaccination.

NATIONAL, STATE AND SCHOOL HOLIDAYS

- January 1: New Year's Day
- January 26: Australia Day
- 2nd Monday in March: Labour Day (Victorian state holiday)
- Good Friday
- Easter Monday
- April 25: Anzac Day
- 2nd Monday in June: Queen's Birthday
- September: Friday before the AFL Grand Final
- 1st Tuesday in November: Melbourne Cup
- December 25: Christmas Day
- December 26: Christmas holiday
- School summer holidays are from mid-December to late January—transportation, accommodations and tourist facilities are heavily booked at this time.

NEWSPAPERS

- The national daily newspaper is *The Australian;* read *The Australian Financial Review* for business news.
- The city's daily newspapers are *The Age*, giving a reasonable coverage of international news, and *The Herald Sun,* a tabloid-style paper.

RADIO

Melbourne has many radio stations, ranging from local community stations RRR and PBS, to FM rock music broadcasters such as Triple J-FM and Triple M-FM, to the Australian Broadcasting Corporation's (ABC) Radio National. There are also many AM music, chat and news stations.

TELEPHONES

- Public telephones are found at phone booths, post offices, hotels, petrol stations, shops, rail and bus stations.
- Local calls cost 50¢ for unlimited time.
- Long-distance calls within Australia, known as STD calls, vary in price, but you should have a good supply of 50¢, A$1 and A$2 coins.
- Call 1800 738 377 for reverse-charge calls.
- Call 1234 for directory assistance.

TOURIST INFORMATION

- City of Melbourne Visitor Information Centre
- ✉ 224 Swanston Street
- ☎ 9658 9658;
melbournetouristinformation.com
- ⏰ Mon–Fri 8–6

POST OFFICES AND POSTAGE

● Post offices are generally open Mon–Fri 9–5. Melbourne General Post Office hours are Mon–Fri 8.15–5.30, Sat 9–5.
● Larger post offices sell airmails, and provide fax and email facilities.
● Stamps can also be purchased in some hotels and from some newsagents and souvenir shops.

ADVICE

● If you experience a theft or any other incident, report it to your hotel and the police. If your traveler's checks are stolen, tell the relevant organization.
● It is safe to drink tap water.
● The only medical problems you are likely to experience are sunburn and mosquito bites.
● For sun protection, make sure you wear sunblock, sunglasses, a hat and long sleeves.
● Dangerous currents can cause problems in the sea in summer. Swim only at beaches with lifeguards, swim between the flags and observe any posted warnings.
● If you undertake long hikes, let someone know of your expected return time.

● Phonecards come in values of A\$5 to A\$50; credit cards can be used from some phones.
● International calls, known as ISD calls, can be made from your hotel and certain public telephones by dialing 0011, followed by the country codes: UK 44; US and Canada 1; France 33; Germany 49.
● To call a Melbourne or Victoria number from outside the state, use the prefix 03. Calls from within the state require no prefix.

TELEVISION

● ABC (Australian Broadcasting Corporation) Channel 2 has no commercials.
● Melbourne has four commercial stations: Channels 7, Nine, Ten and SBS (Special Broadcasting Service). Channel 7 has two sister channels, 7Two and 7Mate. Network Nine's sister channels include Go!, Gem and eXtra. Network Ten's sister station is Channel Eleven. SBS has SBS2, SBS Three and NITV, the National Indigenous Station. Melbourne also has a local community station, Channel 31.
● Cable and satellite services are available in most major hotels.

TOILETS

There is access to free public toilets in parks, public places, galleries, museums, department stores and also in bus and rail stations.

VISITORS WITH DISABILITIES

People with mobility-related impairments have a number of options for getting around in Melbourne. Many taxis have wheelchair access and the more modern trams and buses have wheelchair access and special seating. There are a number of accessible toilets, which meet current Australian Standards. Many attractions and sporting venues accommodate visitors with mobility-related impairments. All parks provide wheelchair-accessible paths and some also have accessible toilets. Search for mobility maps on the City of Melbourne website: melbourne.vic.gov.au.

Language

Most people understand the greeting "G'day" as being Australian slang for "hello." But there are lots of other less familiar words and phrases that you might not recognize when talking with the locals. Australians sometimes say several words as one "waddayareckon" ("what do you reckon?") and "owyagoin" ("how are you going?"). This can be confusing, but you will soon get used to it. Listed here are the meanings of some of the words and phrases you're most likely to hear.

AUSSIE ENGLISH

amber fluid	beer	larrikin	lout, mischievous
ankle biter	small or young child	lollies	candy, sweets
		pommie	English person
arvo	afternoon	rack off	go away, get lost
barney	argument, fight	sanger	sandwich
big smoke	the city	sheila	girl, woman
bloke	man	skite	boast, brag
bonza	excellent, attractive	slab	carton of 24 beer cans
bush	the country	stoked	very pleased
chinwag	chat, conversation	struth!	exclamation of surprise
cobber	mate, friend	stubby	small bottle of beer
dunny	outside toilet		
fair dinkum	real, genuine, true	sunnies	pair of sunglasses
		tee up	to organize something
full as a boot	intoxicated	tinnie	can of beer
get stuffed	go away	true blue	genuine
hard yakka	hard work	tucker	food
hooroo	goodbye	yarn	story
knock off	to steal something, a counterfeit product	yonks	long period of time

Timeline

The Aboriginal people of the Port Phillip area lived in harmony with nature and by their traditional means for thousands of years before European settlement. The nearly 40 different tribal groups throughout present-day Victoria are descendants of people who made their way to the Australian mainland from Southeast Asia up to 60,000 years ago, and led a seminomadic existence. Hunting and gathering for sustenance, the people were bonded to their surroundings by a complex system of spiritual beliefs, and their lives were governed by cultural codes handed down through the generations.

40,000–60,000 years ago
Aboriginal people arrive from Southeast Asia; invent airfoil and fire-based land management.

1770 English navigator Captain James Cook and the *Endeavour* arrive in Botany Bay.

1787 The First Fleet departs from England.

1803 The British send ships to Port Phillip Bay to prevent French settlement.

1835 John Batman negotiates passage through Port Phillip Bay and later claims to have bought it from the local Aboriginal people. Two years later, the site is renamed Melbourne, after the British prime minister.

1851 Gold is discovered near Ballarat. People flock to the city and Melbourne's population multiplies rapidly. The colony of Victoria separates from New South Wales.

1861 The first Melbourne Cup is run.

1883 The first railway service begins between Melbourne and Sydney.

From left to right: Captain James Cook (1728–79); gold nuggets, panned during the Klondike gold rush; Shrine of Remembrance; Old Parliament House; Qantas, the national airline of Australia

1901 The Commonwealth of Australia is proclaimed, joining the six Australian colonies into a federation; the first Commonwealth Parliament opens in Melbourne.

1918 World War I ends. Sixty thousand Australians have died.

1927 Federal Parliament opens in Canberra.

1929 The Great Depression begins.

1939 Black Friday bush fires kill 71 people in Victoria.

1939–45 Australian troops fight overseas during World War II; more than 35,000 die.

1956 First television broadcast in Melbourne. The city hosts the XVI Olympiad.

1967 Indigenous Australians achieve citizenship after nearly 200 years of discrimination.

1971 Neville Bonner becomes the first Indigenous Senator.

1973 Whitlam Government dismantles last remnants of White Australia policy.

1985 *Neighbours* airs for the first time.

1994 Native Title Bill becomes law.

2008 Prime Minister Kevin Rudd apologizes to the Indigenous Australian Stolen Generation.

2010 Victorian Julia Gillard becomes Australia's first female prime minister.

2015 Australia debuts at Eurovision.

2017 Marriage Equality legislated.

BOOM OR BUST

From the time of the gold rush onward, and culminating in the Great Exhibition of 1888, the city of Melbourne enjoyed boom times created by the state's enormous mineral wealth. However, the bubble burst in the 1890s and the period of great economic depression that followed ruined numerous speculators and brought great hardship to many.

NEED TO KNOW TIMELINE

Index

Melbourne 25 Best

WRITTEN BY Rod Ritchie and Julie Walkden
UPDATED BY Lou McGregor
SERIES EDITOR Clare Ashton
COVER DESIGN Jessica Gonzalez
DESIGN WORK Liz Baldin
COLOR REPROGRAPHICS Ian Little

Published in the United Kingdom by AA Publishing.

ISBN 978-1-6409-7203-2

SECOND EDITION

Printed and bound in China by 1010 Printing Group Limited

10 9 8 7 6 5 4 3 2 1

A05671
Maps in this title produced from mapping data supplied by Global Mapping, Brackley, UK © Global Mapping and data available from openstreetmap.org © under the Open Database License found at opendatacommons.org
Transport map © Communicarta Ltd, UK

We would like to thank the following photographers, companies and picture libraries for their assistance in the preparation of this book.

All images are copyright AA/Bill Bachman, except:

6bc AA/John Freeman; 6br Peter Dunphy/Tourism Victoria; 7cl AA/Clive Sawyer; 7cc Tim Webster/Tourism Victoria; 7bc Peter Dunphy/Tourism Victoria; 7br Peter Dunphy/Tourism Victoria; 10/11 Photodisc; 10/11b Visit Victoria; 14bcr Photodisc; Visit Victoria/Alison Mayfield; 16tr Visit Victoria/ Robert Blackburn; 16c Victor Fraile/Alamy; 16cb Visit Victoria/Impress Air; 16/7 Space Hotel, Melbourne; 17tl Visit Victoria/Mark Chew; 17cl Visit Victoria/Robert Blackburn; 17bcl Scienceworks/Ben Healley; 18tr Visit Victoria/Robert Blackburn; 18cbr Visit Victoria/Mark Chew; 18br Visit Victoria/ Robert Seba; 20 Visit Victoria/Julian Kingma; 24tr David Hannah/Tourism Victoria; 26tl OMG upstairs National Trust of Australia (Victoria); 26tc National Trust of Australia (Victoria); 26tr National Trust of Australia (Victoria); 27 OMG upstairs National Trust of Australia (Victoria); 29 State Library of Victoria; 30bl Media Unit - Tourism Victoria; 30bl Visit Victoria/Mark Chew; 30br Visit Victoria/Josie Withers; 31b Visit Victoria/Josie Withers; 34-35t Mark Chew/Tourism Victoria; 36-37t Tourism Victoria; 37c Mark Chew/Tourism Victoria; 38t Mark Chew/Tourism Victoria; 39 Peter Dunphy/Tourism Victoria; 42l Peter Dunphy/Tourism Victoria; 42/43c Peter Dunphy/Tourism Victoria; 43c Mark Chew/Tourism Victoria; 44/5 Visit Victoria/Robert Blackburn; 44tr Visit Victoria/Robert Blackburn; 44cr Visit Victoria/Robert Blackburn; 46tl Peter Dunphy/Tourism Victoria; 46tr Peter Dunphy/Tourism Victoria; 47tl Immigration Museum; 50t Mark Chew/Tourism Victoria; 51c Tourism Victoria; 52 Mark Chew/Tourism Victoria; 53 Peter Dunphy/Tourism Victoria; 56tl Peter Dunphy/Tourism Victoria; 56tr Tourism Victoria; 57tl Peter Dunphy/ Tourism Victoria; 57tr Peter Dunphy/Tourism Victoria; 58 Peter Dunphy/ Tourism Victoria; 59t AA/Adrian Baker; 59cl Visit Victoria/Robert Blackburn; 59cr Peter Dunphy/Tourism Victoria; 60/1 Royal Botanic Gardens; 61tr Royal Botanic Gardens; 61cr Royal Botanic Gardens; 62tl Peter Dunphy/Tourism Victoria; 64b National Trust of Australia (Victoria); 65t Mark Chew/Tourism Victoria; 66t Visit Victoria/Mark Chew; 67t Tourism Victoria; 68t Mark Chew/ Tourism Victoria; 72tl Visit Victoria/Josie Withers; 72tr AA/Adrian Baker; 73tl David Hannah/Tourism Victoria; 74b Visit Victoria/Emily Fitzgerald; 77t Mark Chew/Tourism Victoria; 77c Tourism Victoria; 78t Mark Chew/ Tourism Victoria; 82tl White Studios/Tourism Victoria; 82tr Visit Victoria/ Josie Withers; 84/5 Melbourne Museum, Jennifer McNair; 85tr Visit Victoria/ Lynton Crabb; 85cr Melbourne Museum; 88 Mark Chew/Tourism Victoria; 89 Tourism Victoria; 90 Mark Chew/Tourism Victoria; 94tl Heide Museum of Modern Art Collection; Commissioned through the Heide Foundation with significant; assistance from Lindsay and Paula Fox 2005; Photographer: John Gollings 2006; © Inge King & John Gollings; 94tr Architect: O'Connor + Houle Architecture; Photographer: John Gollings 2006; © John Gollings; 96tr National Trust of Australia (Victoria); 98tl Scienceworks/Scott Parker; 96tr Scienceworks/Dianna Snape; 99b Visit Victoria/Robert Seba; 104t Mark Chew/Tourism Victoria; 105t Tourism Victoria; 106 Mark Chew/Tourism Victoria; 108-112t AA/Clive Sawyer; 108tr Stockbyte Royalty Free; 108tcr Stockbyte Royalty Free; 108bcr Mark Chew/Tourism Victoria; 123 AA/ Christine Osborne; 124bl AA; 124bcr Visit Victoria/Robert Seba; 124cl AA/ Chris Coe; 125bl AA/Adrian Baker; 125br AA/Mike Langford.

Titles in the Series

place, and mood, and how to
...erstand the depth of personal
...iting and remarkable read."

—Joanna Trollope, author of *Other People's Children*

"A sensuous, devoted piece of work that works hard to evoke French domesticity and later the headily foreign atmosphere of colonial Vietnam." —*The Miami Herald*

"[An] evocative, erotic and enjoyable story."
—*The Sunday Telegraph* (London)

"A marvelous achievement, a historical novel that reads less like an invention than like a discovery, a love story that has sprung to life of its own accord from an old trunk. Graceful, subtle and vivid."
—Paul LaFarge, author of *Haussmann, or the Distinction*

"Romantic. . . . Echoes of both *Madame Bovary* and Kate Chopin's *The Awakening* suffuse a nevertheless inventive and artfully composed delineation of a beguiling and complicated woman's arduous journey toward self-understanding. A subtly textured fourth novel: Texier's best yet."
—*Kirkus Reviews*

"Elegant and affecting." —*Scotland on Sunday*

"Elegant as a pair of satin gloves, Catherine Texier's *Victorine* is the enchanting narrative of a unique woman. . . . This is a seductive work of art."
—Diana Abu-Jaber, author of *Crescent*